ACCLAIM FOR
MENNONITE MEETS MR. RIGHT

"Paul Shaffer, the noted theologian/TV sidekick, once said that if God is the ultimate being, he must have the ultimate sense of humor. To which I add, Rhoda Janzen is not far behind. This is one funny book. Not to mention thought-provoking and touching."

—AJ Jacobs, author of *The Year of Living Biblically*

"Three stars! Breezy despite the weighty subject matter... Janzen's wit and love of fashion keep things light, but her conversion to Pentecostalism after a miraculous return to health sends the book into serious seekers' territory."   —*People*

"Hilarious...Janzen is the kind of writer—world-weary yet incredulous; girlfriend-esque and conversational—that draws you along through a story with ease. This book is an easy read for a fall weekend. You'll be rooting for the author the whole way. The book would fit naturally on a shelf, say, next to your collection of beat-up Anne Lamott paperbacks. It has that same sort of accessibility to it; that same sort of acceptance...It's terrific to see all these memorable characters [from *Mennonite in a Little Black Dress*], a bit farther down the road. And it's great that Janzen, for all her life has changed, can still make them as humorous as ever. And not only them: herself."   —*Buffalo News*

"[A] vibrant, charming narrative."   —*Publishers Weekly*

"Rhoda Janzen is one of the few people I trust to write about faith without using God to clobber me. She writes about the most serious things in the world—life, death, family, love—with such spot-on honesty, spiritual humility, and disarming humor that I would follow her anywhere. The nicest thing I can say about her new book is that it made me want to be a better person. It is that good."

—Barbara Brown Taylor, author of *An Altar in the World* and *Leaving Church*

"Given the gravity of the subjects—cancer and religious conversion—Janzen gave herself an enormous challenge. Could she maintain her hallmark comic voice in the midst of suffering and transformation? The answer is yes, and that is no small accomplishment...What makes a memoir great is the honesty to claim what has been right in front of oneself all along. Only when we are ready for truth to sink in can it become our own. The excitement of discovery is palpable in this book."

—*Christian Century*

"[Janzen has] an uproarious, bawdy sense of humor, great comedic timing and what in her hands seems to be a wacky life."

—*Minneapolis Star-Tribune*

"A delight for fans of [Janzen's] warm, wisecracking style... Honest and remarkably funny...Janzen writes of her newfound faith like a travel writer discovering an exotic new pocket of the world, and her enthusiasm and spirit and knack for finding humor in the God details make this book a crowd-pleaser."

—*Miami Herald*

"A very funny writer...A heartfelt memoir that is both hilarious and inspiring." —*Great Day Houston*

"Janzen is pointing toward the value of examining one's own beliefs, whatever they may be, and finding a way to live with them in joy. And if, along the way, you discover that a man who uses a bow and arrow to dispatch a hungry raccoon that comes in through the kitchen cat door can also be capable of the greatest tenderness and devotion, so much the better." —*Tampa Bay Times*

"Smart and witty...Janzen has a remarkable ability to demystify religion through humor and humanity." —*Columbus Dispatch*

"MENNONITE MEETS MR. RIGHT made me laugh out loud, often enough to make my beloved children inquire as to whether I was losing my mind. Too much spiritual writing these days claims that religious practice is about healing or developing the self. But Rhoda Janzen avoids this theme: here she sets out on a path to become more loving, grateful, and helpful to *others*. This is particularly impressive given that she's writing about a period in her life when she's got a scary, life-threatening illness, and a brand-new family. Bravo, Rhoda—or rather, 'Thank God!'" —Kate Braestrup, author of *Here if You Need Me* and *Beginner's Grace*

ALSO BY RHODA JANZEN

Mennonite in a Little Black Dress

Mennonite Meets Mr. Right

—— ❧ ——

a memoir of faith, hope, and love

Rhoda Janzen

GRAND CENTRAL
PUBLISHING

NEW YORK   BOSTON

for Timothy Ray Burton

Grand Central Publishing
Hachette Book Group
237 Park Avenue
New York, NY 10017

www.HachetteBookGroup.com

Printed in the United States of America

RRD-C

Originally published in hardcover by Grand Central Publishing as *Does This Church Make Me Look Fat?*

First Trade Edition: October 2013
10 9 8 7 6 5 4 3 2 1

Grand Central Publishing is a division of Hachette Book Group, Inc. The Grand Central Publishing name and logo is a trademark of Hachette Book Group, Inc.

The Hachette Speakers Bureau provides a wide range of authors for speaking events. To find out more, go to www.hachettespeakersbureau.com or call (866) 376-6591.

The publisher is not responsible for websites (or their content) that are not owned by the publisher.

Library of Congress Control Number: 2012940706

ISBN 978-1-4555-0287-5 (pbk.)

CONTENTS

Stella's House

Having divorced after a fifteen-year marriage, and having returned in a scattershot way to the dating scene, I naturally had limited faith in my judgment. So when I found myself falling for a Jesus-nail-necklace-wearing manly man, the kind whose hands were so huge they ripped his jeans pockets, I thought my common sense was all a-pother.

Working against me was the fact that I am an egghead intellectual. Have you noticed that sometimes scholars do one tiny thing really well, but at the expense of more important things? For instance, I can diagram any sentence from the late fiction of Henry James. Why anybody would want me to is a mystery, but you'd be surprised at how many requests I get. We're talking about sentences that march on and on, to and fro, like a bewildered Energizer bunny. I have limited life-management skills, yet I can diagram these sentences with the speed of an idiot savant. Why is it necessary to diagram *any* sentence? you ask. Good question!

Advanced education doesn't make one wise. In fact—stay

with me here—what if having a PhD makes you a tomfool? I can think of lots of evidence for this, and not just me. Consider the overeducated grad student I once met at an LA industry party. This chap was writing his dissertation on the iconic significance of Mr. Peanut. I am not making this up. The fellow shared with me many of the important cultural developments surrounding the meteoric rise of Mr. Peanut circa 1916. He traced the class implications of Mr. Peanut's spats, top hat, cane, and monocle. Just when I thought I could take no more, I spotted a willowy supermodel type in a one-shouldered clingy aubergine tunic. She was carrying a tremendous red onion as an accessory to her outfit. And she was holding it very casually in the palm of one hand, like a tiny evening bag, as if carrying a big red onion conferred a status that she was too modest to comment on. Lalala, no biggie, it's an onion! I encouraged the dissertation guy to go introduce himself to her, but he got shy. I was, like, "Don't be a ninny! March right up to that onion hottie and tell her what you know about Mr. Peanut!"

My new boyfriend would never have uttered a single comment upon the iconic significance of Mr. Peanut. Nor would he have attended a cocktail party. Mitch was sober. He didn't drink, he didn't smoke, he didn't swear. His vocabulary could have passed muster with toddlers and kittens. He looked tough with his shaved head and scary biceps, but his language was clean as a whistle.

Out of respect for this man's unusual and valiant restraint, I was trying to clean up my act. This was a challenge for a potty-mouthed professor who felt that she had paid her vocabulary dues and could with impunity utter any four-letter word in the English language.

I expected that, as the relationship progressed, I'd start to see slips and cracks in Mitch's language—a four-letter word here, an obscenity there. Mitch had been a card-carrying hoodlum, and a drug-dealer, and also once he had gotten fired from a bussing job for stealing the servers' tips. Impressed, I said, "Can I tell my sister that you mouthed off to an officer when he busted you for stealing his jacket?"

"Sure."

"Can I mention that you sold weed out of your backyard and planted pipe bombs in people's mailboxes?"

He answered in his slow drawl, "That's just the plain truth. You can say any of that."

Mitch had been the kind of alcoholic who drove stinking drunk, with open bottles in the car. Then he found the Lord, who miraculously sobered him up. But the Lord didn't clean up Mitch's language. Mitch had to do that by himself. For a whole year he spent the noon hour at work biting his tongue in the lunchroom, saying nothing rather than risk the stream of foul language that had characterized his conversation before Christ. These lunchroom descriptions intrigued me. Sometimes profanity seems the outcropping of a limited imagination: "Eff the effers! Somebody effed up the effin microwave with some effin ravioli!" I'd like to think that Mitch was more resourceful.

Mitch had overhauled his vocabulary, sure enough. Still, after almost two months of dating, one might expect the occasional outburst. So far Mitch's spiciest utterance had been, "Well, I'll be double-dipped!" Imagine this in a light southern accent, coming from a huge goateed rocker who has a permit to carry a concealed weapon. When a man has a gun in his pants, you don't expect him to be double-dipped.

On an early date to a sculpture garden I asked Mitch why he was always so taciturn. "If a man don't learn to curb his tongue," he said, "he'll talk a lot of foolishness."

We were passing an enormous abstract painted steel sculpture by Alexander Liberman. Struck by the soaring arches and muscular lines, I paused. "What does *that* say to you?"

"Says some dude had a lot of free time."

"But isn't it spectacular?"

"Sure. It's spectacular if you got enough food to feed your kids."

Mitch's way of reducing things to their simplest essence provided a pleasant contrast with the sort of commentary provided in my circles. Literary critics liked to make things as opaque and complicated as possible. English professors chased nuance. Mitch summed things up.

Mitch's sixteen-year-old son Leroy had already confided that for as long as he could remember, his buddies had been terrified of his dad, around whom there had sprung up a stern terminator legend. First there was Mitch's size. Leroy's dad caricatured the impossible male physique—chest like a scenic vista, cannon arms, a waist that disappeared into his jeans like a genie into a bottle. He kept clanking steel gym equipment in his living room.

Then there was the curious catlike walk. He moved with incredible lightness, as if he expected someone to attack him from behind. Anyone who's studied martial arts recognizes that walk. Put him in a suit, he looks like Secret Service. When you put other men in suits, they look like accountants or limo drivers.

Leroy told me that his father's nickname was The Boxer.

I frowned. "I'd hate to be the box."

"Yeah," Leroy returned. "Stealth thinks my dad looks like 'Stone Cold' Steve Austin."

"Stealth?" I asked. "Your friend's name is Stealth?"

"Yeah," said Leroy. "He's not my friend, though. He's my cousin."

"Are you trying to tell me that you have an aunt who named her child Stealth?"

Leroy nodded. "After the bomber."

They seemed a strange family to me.

Mitch's faith had played a central role in his sobriety, and I couldn't help but be impressed that he had so dramatically turned his life around. How many people manage to alter their core character—deliberately, sentiently—as adults? I could list folks who had changed gradually over time, mellowing under the gentle weight of decades. And I could name people who had been strengthened by enduring external events out of their control, such as loss or trauma. But I couldn't name a single person who had managed to transform himself on his own.

In this sense Mitch was a rare bird. When I asked him how he had achieved such a stunning turnaround, he shrugged. "That wasn't me. That was all God."

Yikes. I had grown up in a conservative Mennonite community, and this sort of totalizing religious expression made me uncomfortable. I associated it with foofy needlepoint pillows that said I BELIEVE IN ANGELS, or, in the other direction, giant lawn boards advising neighbors to REPENT, SINNERS!

Some of the church folk in my community of origin referred to me as *abgefallen*, "fallen away." True enough, my life as an adult didn't look very much like theirs. Yet *abgefallen* is a term I never would have applied to myself because I've always loved my Mennonite roots, my family, and the faith tradition practiced therein. In fact in many ways I still identify culturally and theologically as a Mennonite.

It wasn't the life of the mind that led me away from the Mennonites, but rather my overinvestment in it. I began challenging and inquiring, as young scholars do, anxious to be and seem smart. Now, after two decades in academia, I still believed in God. That is, I thought there was a benevolent force at work in the universe.

Occasionally on Sunday mornings I'd drop by an Episcopal service. Episcopal politics matched mine. I liked the Episcopal music, too. Most of the hymns were familiar to me, but the services also featured some long tuneless pieces of chanted music that sounded suspiciously as if somebody had made them up in the car on the way to church. And if the Episcopalians needed more to recommend them, there was the pleasantly high-church smell that issued from the busy little thurible of incense. If you smelled anything in my Mennonite church of origin, it was an old-lady perfume such as Avon's Here's My Heart. My brother used to detect this familiar fragrance on many a raccoon collar, and in the general hum before the service, he would risk in a quick falsetto: "Here's My Fart!"

Perhaps in the loosest sense you could say that in my adult

life I was *abgefallen*. But if I was, it wasn't because I had set out to defy the church or to reject God. I just wanted to move toward the ineluctable glamour of red onions.

Mitch had told me to save Saturday, all of Saturday, for a jaunt up north. It was hot for an autumn day, and although the leaves had started to turn, we drove with the windows down, the sun burning our shoulders. Whenever Mitch drove, he spread his big hand over my thigh, as if his hand belonged there by right and invitation.

"You want some sunscreen?" he asked, nodding to the backseat. Beside a canvas tote stuffed haphazardly with towels and 25 SPF, an old-fashioned Coleman aluminum ice chest made me smile. Once I had owned such a cooler, a hand-me-down from my parents, a big creaky red one that hinted at camp stoves and fried potatoes. I had always had a glad spot in my heart for a big embarrassing ice chest. Now I looked sidelong at Mitch. He didn't seem embarrassed at all. Well, why would he be, given the gym equipment in the living room?

"Nice cooler," I said.

"That was my dad's. I found it out in the woodshed. Thought you'd like it—it's old school! Look inside."

I peeped under the lid. Fresh fruit, deli turkey, cut-up veggies, dark chocolate. Perfect.

"Where are we going?" I asked.

"It's a surprise."

Two hours later, when Mitch pulled into the parking lot at Northern WaterCraft, I was delighted. I'd never been kayaking before. A bus would take us out to the boats, we would work the river until we got tired, and then another bus would come to fetch us back at either the two-, three-, or four-hour landings. "Let's go for the whole four hours," I said, confident in my lean muscle mass. "We'll slather on the sunscreen."

The sun was climbing, and it was getting hotter by the minute. Around us, would-be kayakers were wiping their brows, crowding into the shade under the only awning. One noisy group was already passing a bottle of Jack Daniel's back and forth, pouring shots into insulated mugs. It was 10:30 a.m. Mitch and I smiled at each other, goofy within the circle of our private attraction. I reached out and lightly touched the tiny patch of graying hair under his lower lip. "I'm glad we won't be having a Jack Daniel's kinda day," I whispered.

He cupped my chin in his hand and kissed me exactly as if we weren't in full view of fifty sets of eyes.

"Excuse me." An older woman approached us, granddaughter in tow. The woman was wearing a tank top that said, MY CAIRN TERRIER IS SMARTER THAN YOUR HONOR STUDENT. "Me and my friends were watching you two, and we wanna know something."

Mitch had backed away from the kiss, but his sweaty arm still hung loosely around my shoulders. The woman put a conversational hand on his other biceps. "Ask away," Mitch invited.

Her soda can smelled like beer. "Me and my friends wanna know if you two are married. We figured you couldn't be married, not with the way you keep looking at each other..." Her voice trailed off apologetically.

"No," said Mitch. "We're not married."

"I knew it!" the woman exclaimed, raising her soda to her friends under the awning. They clapped and woohooed. "Kiss her again!" somebody shouted. Mitch tipped me back off balance, sweeping me into one of those fifties Hollywood clinches. The ladies under the awning cheered.

It wasn't hard to stay afloat in the kayak, but you had to navigate carefully. If you hit an exposed root, or another kayaker, over you went. We saw many such mishaps in the first hour, when the river was still crowded with boaters who were just starting to drink—men yelling at their wives, women drenched and plump, clinging to their kayaks as swift currents whisked them downstream. "I can't get UP!" one woman shouted. "Eff you, Milo!"

After the second landing the river began thinning out. Most of the revelers were too drunk to go on, though we did pass a party who had beached their kayaks on the rocky shore. They were sitting on the grass, clustered together. One of their number, too tipsy to know better, had crept back toward the river. As we rounded the point, she crouched down bare-bottomed, shorts around her ankles, urinating in full view of her friends and of us. Her pale posterior looked like a curly white grub. It was clear she meant to pee into the river, but she was flooding her shorts.

"Whitney!" shouted one of her friends, waving. "Whitney, show us your boobs!"

Whitney obligingly lifted her T-shirt and removed one breast from a sports bra. She twiddled it as if much surprised to see it there beneath her shirt.

"Whiiiiiiiitttttttttnnnnnneeeyyyyy!" came the woman's call as the current swept us on, "I like your boobs, Whitney!" She was almost sobbing now. "I wish I had your boobs, Whitney!"

After Whitney and her friends, we saw only one other party. Two canoes full of middle-aged men lay in ambush under birches that drooped low over the water, their canoes poised on opposite banks. Because of their raucous laughter, we assumed that they were taking a break for liquid refreshment. They weren't. Suddenly their leader addressed me in a loud bellicose voice: "You there, blondie with the ponytail! Notre Dame or Michigan State?"

To me all team sports are irrational jingoism. But I gamely called back, "Notre Dame!"

"Hell, no!" roared the man, a big fiftyish guy with hair spilling from his tank top. "Wrong answer! Get 'em!" Both canoes promptly attacked us with water cannons at the ready. "Get her shirt wet!" "Get his hair!" "Notre Dame is going DOWN!"

Soon after this interlude, we passed the three-hour landing. After that we saw no one. Alone with the silvery dip of our paddles, we settled into pleasurable silence. Why speak? Waves of cicadas shrilled, and the air was heavy with lopseed and wild mint. Ninebark and silky dogwood hung like children over the banks, trailing their fingers in the water. Sometimes we caught sight of a cabin or a staircase built down the steep embankment, but the current moved us so swiftly that we couldn't absorb the picture of these hidden getaways. When the channel was wide enough, we held hands in our separate kayaks, sometimes for ten minutes at a time, adrift on the fierce bright water. At other times I paddled ahead, my arm slowly moving into the fourth hour of dipping, a delicious fatigue steeling the muscles deep in my shoulders. Always I could feel Mitch at my back, his eyes watching my progress as I cut through the water.

Once the tip of my kayak caught a submerged log, and I capsized before I knew what was happening. The chill swirl sucked the kayak and the oar from my astonished hands, and I barely had time to grab them before the rapids pulled me past the log. I seized the bare end of the kayak, hanging on, and with a mighty push hoisted my torso up out of the water. My skirt blossomed restlessly around me, wide like a lotus.

Mitch saw me go down, but he couldn't stop. "I'll wait for you!" he shouted back over his shoulder, disappearing around a bend. There was no turning around in this current. By the time I made it to the riverbank, the water had propelled me all the way to the elbow around which Mitch had disappeared. I got back in my kayak, shoved off with my oar, and congratulated myself on my waterproof Merrills. Sweeping around the bend, I saw Mitch, dripping wet from cap to shoes, standing onshore, holding out a huge branch. Awwww shucks, I thought—he was planning on saving me! I grabbed his branch and let him haul me in. We kissed frantically, like teens in bleachers. But something happened while I hung on to him, stumbling over the solid branch he had stretched out to me—something that felt scripted, prearranged, inevitable. Suddenly the spirit of delicate adventure that had perfused the outing was gone. We stood there staring at each other like idiots.

I whispered, "This feels—so—so—"

"Real?" he asked.

I nodded dumbly.

This snippet of dialogue on the riverbank was more than the

sum of its parts, and we both knew it. We didn't have passionate sex in the hawthorn. We didn't declare anything. We didn't
change our course as we paddled the stretch to the last landing.
We didn't reveal new intimacies as we waited for the pick-up
bus, even when we became aware of a small but noisy group
clustered ahead. How they had paddled for four hours through
steady drinking was a mystery, but I took my hat off to them, especially to one cowboy who stood proud as a bantam in a teensy
green sequined bikini bottom and boots.

"Don't look now," I said, "but there's a guy up there wearing
nothing but boots and emerald sequined boy shorts. Once I saw
Axl Rose wearing wee velveteen shorts onstage. You'd think his
friends would have said something."

Emerald Panties looked about thirty-five, straight with a
droopy moustache, and somehow deeply at peace with the way
his love handles were squeezing out of his small sparkly bikini
bottom. Mitch chuckled. "Dude's got it going *on*. Take it like
you own it! Treat it like a rental!"

"Can you think of any circumstances that would persuade
you to wear emerald sparkly manpanties?" I asked.

"Sure," he said.

This astonished me. Mitch seemed awfully manly. He was
downright monosyllabic, with a fifty-gallon air compressor in
his garage. He made chili from a seasoning packet for Sunday
dinner. I had heard him express interest in shooting the kitsch
rhinoceros that unicycled on a tightrope high above diners at
The Piper, a local restaurant. But meanwhile I considered the
picture of my big bald terminator in sparkly green manpanties.
Festive!

I nodded, impressed. "Care to elaborate?"

"I'd wear that green thing if somebody would give $5,000 to Stella's House."

Stella's House was a way station for Moldovan orphans in transition, one of Mitch's favorite charities.

"Would you accept $4,000? To teach those poor girls typing skills?"

"I guess, yeah."

"$3,000? And you can't tell anyone that you're wearing the green manpanties for the glory of your Savior?"

"Okay, $3,000," he said finally. I could see I had pushed him to his limit. "But I'm not wearing those sissified boots. Dude looks like a lady."

On the long drive home we ate rolled-up turkey and little chunks of tepid watermelon, rotating our shoulders and complaining about our sore delts. In spite of the prosaic conversation, I was pretty sure that the drenched moment onshore had ushered in a new phase for the relationship. Oh, he didn't say it. What he actually said was, "Do you have some floss?" And what I actually answered was, "You can't floss while you're driving, are you insane?"

But that's not what we meant. What we were really saying was this.

"I am falling in love with you."

"How strange and surprising is the human heart!"

TWO

⁂

Lady Problems

Leroy was involved in a dynamic youth program at Mitch's church. When I was Leroy's age, I hated church activities with a cavalier contempt illustrated by Regency romances. These tales abound with Bow Street Runners, impoverished but genteel governesses, and exciting duels at dawn. Luckily the books in this genre are all identical, and therefore they repeat a truly uplifting moment. This is when the black sheep viscount leisurely slaps his glove across the villain's chin. How eloquent, how civilized! I longed for the rebel chops to slap our youth group's chin.

On Wednesday evenings before church I sat in obedient silence at my mother's dinner table, dreading the evening that lay ahead. Although I was more Mennonite doormat than naughty viscount, I did a nice eyeroll-lipcurl combination that said, if anyone was listening, "Down with thin content, teen drama, and bad shoes!" When my youth group peers, eyes glassy and sincere, swayed to the tune of "It Only Takes a Spark to Get a Fire Going," I'd curl my lip, like the viscount. Moist groupthink!

Thus I marveled that Mitch's son was eager to attend Never Enough, Mitch's church's youth program. Leroy found this program inspiring. The kids designed funky NEVER ENOUGH T-shirts. They choreographed praise dances in which they dressed like zombies. The teens always had a narrative about how the zombies represented their lives before conversion to Christ, but I suspected that the kids just wanted to dress up like monsters and lurch around. On Wednesday nights Leroy couldn't get to church fast enough.

Mitch had experienced his own version of disaffected youth, so he was thrilled that his son actually *wanted* to go to church. Moreover, Mitch himself was deeply committed to this church. That is, he wasn't like one of those dadpant oldsters who insisted on going to church for the sake of pious religiosity. Rather, there was something about *this* church that Mitch loved. He loved the pastor, the people, the worship. He loved the teaching, the service programs, the bake sales. It was clear to me that this church was an expression of his core values. If I was to keep dating him, I would need to see what it was all about.

Although Mitch never asked me to come with him, I knew that it would be meaningful to him if I did. Checking out a guy's church would be an intermediate step between closing a restaurant in pleasurable tête à tête and meeting the boyfriend's family. In fact visiting a guy's church *was* a form of meeting the family, since these church folk apparently supported one another with prayer chains, moving trucks, and pie. During my growing-up years my pastor father had been invited to speak in hundreds of churches, crossing many denominational borders. Over the years I saw many styles of worship. I sang, I bowed, I knelt. I ate barbecued beans at many a potluck. The thought of a Pentecostal service didn't faze me. I expected, maybe, some ebullient hand clapping. So I took a deep breath and gave myself a drumroll, a church drumroll, with a bad snare drum, the kind that goes *tsss*.

"Can I wear pants?" I asked Mitch. "The God of my youth insisted on long dowdy prairie skirts."

"God don't care what you wear."

When Mitch came to pick me up, I modeled my church-lady outfit for him, a dark fitted skirt-suit with high closed pumps. "Does this church make me look fat?" I asked.

"Relax already," he said. "It ain't a law firm."

The church was neat without being excessive in the Jim-and-Tammy-Faye kind of way. Nobody was wearing too much makeup. I did see a lot of tall hair, but then I live in Michigan. The woman behind me was wearing skintight snakeskin pleather pants and tomato platform stilettos, as if purchased from a catalogue for transvestites. I tried to picture her in a Mennonite service. Maybe Mennonites needed Drag Queen Day to loosen things up, in the spirit of school celebrations such as Western Day and Clash Day.

Suddenly enormous curtains swooshed open at the front of the church, with an assertive musical fanfare, as in a show. Onstage eight vocalists fronted a full band. I was astounded when the pastor later referred to these vocalists, who were mostly Hispanic and African-American, as the Praise & Worship Minstrels. The Minstrels had chosen to wear shades of turquoise and black, and, like the full choir I would see on future Sundays, were united in a complex choreography. Brother Vern, whom I would grow to love, looked like a sixties backup singer for The

Temptations. These folks were getting their praise on, turning and swaying and snapping.

Dancing! In church! I had never seen church vocalists do anything but stand up poker-straight in sober garments. This group was shaking their thang and waving sparkler pom-poms. The guy in the middle was bent over at the waist, punching the air, working himself up into a holy frenzy. Off to the right three guys on the trumpet, French horn, and sax were also sporting shades of turquoise and black. The guy in front of the sax was praising Jesus in an azure double-breasted six-button suit, cerulean from collar to cuff. In between songs he pressed a handkerchief to a glistening lip.

The Minstrels plunged the congregants into enthusiastic worship. Pentecostals, I learned, don't just clap their hands. They stand up and shout in the middle of the service. They wave colorful banners. They break-dance for Jesus. They sometimes run sprinting around the sanctuary. One dude wandered up to the altar and did a spirit-led interpretive dance. His moves reminded me of the time my mom showed me how to hula-hoop. But, hey, I had to admire his free spirit.

Pentecostals aren't afraid to shake it. In fact they believe that God *wants* them to worship with joyous freedom, dancing and lifting their arms. I loved this idea. If God is who he says he is, why *wouldn't* we want to jump up and get our bodies involved with our hearts? However, it was a couple of Sundays before I had the brass to go stand at the altar with the other happy worshippers. It's hard to override the Mennonite impulse to behave as if I were at a job interview. "How do you do, God? I am prompt, reliable, and computer literate."

When I finally did make my way up to the altar, I stood right next to a guy whose footwork was a river dance of hallelujah. All I did was sway a little, like a redwood acknowledging a breeze.

These Pentecostals favored long, noisy worship sessions in which everybody shouted the song lyrics. Congregants freely picked their own key. The overheads showed lyrics but no notes. Nobody around me was singing in harmony. Nor did the musical selections have verses per se. Instead they repeated a chorus about forty times with ascending volume, never varying the lyric, as in a song I always used to teach to kids I was babysitting if their parents didn't pay me enough:

> You can't ride in my little red wagon!
> The axle's broken and the wheels are draggin'!
> Second verse, same as the first!
> Little bit louder and a LITTLE BIT WORSE!

By the third verse, the children were screaming their little lungs out, and I had my revenge on their cheapo parents. In the Pentecostal church an example of this style of singing would be

> I exalt thee
> I exalt thee
> I exalt thee
> O LORD! *(repeat 40 times)*

Being Mennonite, I was hungry for a little narrative development in my music, a plot of some kind—a problem, an admission, a promise of better times to come. Not so at Mitch's church.

It struck me that this style of worship was very Buddhist, with its determination to inhabit one moment fully. I tried to immerse myself in the tedious repetitions. But I petered out and sat down around the twentieth chorus, when other folks were just getting into the beatific hand waving and torso swaying. Eventually "I Exalt Thee" dissolved into a cacophony of interpretive runs, with the Minstrels shouting and musing, each according to his or her zeitgeist. I had no idea what people were yelling there at the end. But it went on a good while.

In worship these Pentecostals were 100 percent different from the Mennonites of my youth. The latter were sober and buttoned-up. Mennonites can sing in four-part harmony without moving a muscle. If you happen to notice that in worship we resemble certain members of the mentally ill population, rigid and waxy from too much Haldol, well, we're doing it on purpose. If anybody hears a still small word from the Lord, nobody says so. Mennonites believe in the inherent dignity of the gospel, and they downplay all those parts of the New Testament where Jesus acts a little kooky.

But what I immediately liked about the Pentecostals was their willingness to improvise, to be sidetracked by the Spirit. I'd never suffered much from distraction. In my life the Spirit had left me strictly alone, and I don't blame him. When I'm in the zone, I don't even hear the doorbell, let alone the Spirit. Often I sit down at my computer right after my early 6:00 a.m. run, and wham, it's dinnertime. Also, I make lists. Lists imply a certain rigidity, do they not? An unwillingness to depart from the plan?

Sometimes I have even added tasks to a list retroactively, after I have already done them, just for the pleasure of crossing them out. What maker of lists doesn't appreciate a foray into joyous discursivity now and then? To wit: the pastor was trying to make a point about how ineffective we are as Christians if we try to get the job done outside of the context of Christian community. We need to stay plugged in. His train of thought inspired him with an unplanned analogy from the nature channel.

"I forget if this involves tigers or lions," the pastor said. "But the tigers were hunting a wildebeest in a pack. And they surrounded it—"

"Lions!" shouted several congregants, who had seen the show.

"—the lions surrounded it and worked together to take down the wildebeest. These lions helped one another!"

"Yes they did!" shouted a brother. "Amen!"

Mennonites are all about peacemaking, but in this analogy the corporate body of Christ was being compared to a force of savage predation. The hapless wildebeest, a metaphor for Christian service, was a project destroyed rather than created. A fresh comparison from the pulpit! If the pastor had thought out the ramifications of this analogy in his home office as he prepared the sermon, he might not have used it. But then I would not have had the pleasure of envisioning a pride of muscular lions running and prowling on the veldt, or the wildebeest twitching in a pool of blood.

One Sunday afternoon Mitch said in the slight southern drawl that melted me, "You ever been to a healin service?"

"Like evangelists smiting someone on the forehead and shouting 'Be heal-ed!'?" I asked suspiciously.

"Smitin?"

I smote my own forehead by way of illustration, falling back as if struck with the aggressive spirit of tent revivals.

Mitch shook his head. "Nobody's gonna get smote. But who knows what-all you'll see if you come along tonight."

That night the senior pastor invited the elders to come forward. A sober group of middle-aged men made their way down to the front of the church. The pastor explained that this evening the elders would be prayerfully exercising one of the Gifts of the Spirit.

The Gifts of the Spirit aren't the same as the Fruits of the Spirit. As close as I could figure it, when you got filled with the Holy Spirit, these Gifts of the Spirit just inexplicably popped up, like ads on your computer. The Fruits arrived more gradually. The Fruits I recognized from the church of my youth. They were things like joy, love, peace, meekness, long-suffering, etc.—basically, the visible results of the spiritually fit life. In other words, the Fruits provided the evidence of transformative spiritual change. Because my Mennonites had never emphasized the Holy Spirit, I was much less familiar with the Gifts of the Spirit. I wasn't sure what to expect.

The pastor said that the elders would be deploying a specific Gift of the Spirit, the Word of Knowledge. I'd never heard of the Word of Knowledge before. It went like this. Into the ear or heart of an elder the Holy Spirit would whisper the name of a physical complaint suffered by some member of the congregation. The elder would then call out the name of the illness. The congregant who was suffering from this illness would stand, and then everyone would cluster round the pained, the scoliotic, and the cramped. The healthy congregants would lay hands on the sick, and supposedly there would be a miraculous healing.

I was disappointed when the pastor asked the congregation not to speak in tongues—it implied that they usually do at this type of service—but overall I didn't mind swapping the tongues for the Word of Knowledge. Who wouldn't be jazzed about the Word of Knowledge? This seemed like a Protestant equivalent of the Catholic power of absolution, when a priest takes it upon himself to announce that a sinner is forgiven. In both absolution and the Word of Knowledge, we see a bunch of men acting as the special mouthpiece of the Almighty. What's not to love?

After a prayer, a holy hush descended on the congregation. The pastor made the first move, playing to a rustling expectation, as when someone at a karaoke party decides, Dang it! I'm gonna break the ice! "I'm getting something!" the pastor announced. Down below the pulpit, among the clustered elders, he stood at attention, alert to possibility, stiff as an antenna. "Is there anybody in the house who throws up a lot?"

Up springs a hefty brother. "I do!" he shouts. "Praise the Lord!"

"Brother, you say you throw up a lot?"

"I got bronchitis real bad!" calls the brother. "And when I got me a coughing fit, I sometimes throw up!"

"Can I have an amen?" says Pastor.

"AMEN!" shouts the congregation.

"Can we see these illnesses up on the overhead?"

The huge PowerPoint screen suddenly activated, and somewhere a techie swiftly typed, "THROWS UP A LOT." This appeared in giant caps on a heavenly blue background, as if straight from the mouth of God. A verse from Sunday School days suddenly dropped into my head, Daniel 5:5, in which God's disembodied fingers write a prophetic message on King Belshazzar's wall. (Hey! Just like Facebook!) "In the same hour came forth fingers of a man's hand, and wrote over against the candlestick upon the plaster of the wall of the king's palace." I had memorized this verse with pleasure when I was eight, never guessing that it would come in so handy when I was forty-five, sitting agog in my boyfriend's charismatic church. Who wouldn't love the idea that a voice from the Great Beyond was being recorded at the front of the house on a tremendous visual aid? I had never witnessed a nonbiblical divine communication before, let alone a phrase like THROWS UP A LOT on a church overhead.

An elder now beckoned the microphone. He looked as if he was getting something, too. "I'm feeling to say that there's someone here with lady problems!"

"Lady Problems!" echoed the pastor. "How about *Lady Problems*? Can I have *Lady Problems*?" The pastor sounded not unlike Richard Dawson on *Family Feud*, when a family from Pascagoula shouts "Bra!" in answer to the question, "What could you make with a coconut if you were stranded on a desert island?"

A second bullet point appeared on the enormous overhead. Now the screen said:

- THROWS UP A LOT
- LADY PROBLEMS

As the Word of Knowledge went forth, I counted fifty-seven people standing before the laying on of hands started. Of the fifty-seven, twenty-four believers later signaled that they had been healed of their complaints, but the zenith for me was the Power-Point screen. By the end of the evening it included things like:

- SWELLED ANKLE
- ISSUES/PAIN IN RIGHT EAR
- BLOCKAGE

Let's just say that Mitch and I had plenty to talk about on the way home.

A professor's workweek is tight. I often have to schedule student appointments at fifteen-minute intervals to get everybody in. The week after the healing service I was so busy I had to cancel a lunch date with Mitch.

"How come?"

"I have lady problems."

He laughed.

"No, really. They saw something funky on my mammogram and they want me to come in for an ultrasound."

"You worried?"

"Not really. They've called me back before. There's a family history. And the breasts of young women are notoriously difficult to read in mammography. It's just a precaution. I'm way too young to have cancer." I said this with the confidence of one who ran six miles a day and made her own homemade yogurt.

I worked late after the ultrasound. There was a dinner with a visiting writer, a poetry reading, and a forty-five-minute commute, so by the time I got home, it was almost eleven. On my bedside table three messages blinked with a gathering emphasis, as if to say, *J'accuse*! All were from Silvia, my doctor's nurse. First Silvia urged me to call back as soon as possible. Then Silvia emphasized that the doctor needed to discuss the test results with me immediately. Finally, Silvia instructed me to page the doctor no matter what time I returned. I obediently paged my doctor, who was lovely and frank and warm, and who never hurried through appointments.

"Rox," I said. "Sorry to page you so late, but Silvia said it was important. What's going on?"

"You didn't do very well on that test," she said without preamble.

"Hey, I'm a professor," I protested. "Professors *always* do well on tests."

"Not this time."

I sighed. "*D* or *F*?"

"*F−*," Rox said flatly. "We need to get you in for a biopsy tomorrow."

"Can't. I have two seminars, a committee meeting, and a thing. How about Friday?"

"Rhoda," she said patiently, "you're not hearing me. *We need to get you in for a biopsy tomorrow.*"

I sighed. "As long as I can go back to work on Wednesday."

"I'll give you Vicodin and some tiny icepacks with Wonder Woman on them."

"Tempting."

"Wear your loosest bra. Tomorrow at 8:00 a.m. sharp."

Rox didn't perform the biopsy, but it was she who called me on Wednesday, the day after the procedure, toward the end of my office hours. One of my students was in my office. The student was struggling to diagram a sentence that contained a participial phrase inside a gerund. When the phone rang, I motioned for the student to hold her thought. "Sorry," I whispered to the student. "I have to take this."

"Rhoda. We've got the results."

"Good. But can I call you right back? I'm with a student."

"No. No, you may not call me back. Honestly, Rhoda! You have cancer. There's never a good time to hear that, but the sooner you hear it, the sooner we can begin treating it. It's infiltrating ductal carcinoma. It's a big mass, and it's moving fast. I'm referring you to the top breast surgeon in Grand Rapids. She'll do some tests and she'll be able to tell you if the malignancy has metastasized to your lymphatic system. You won't be able to sidestep the chemo. Don't worry—there are amazing new antinausea drugs, so unless you throw up a lot as an adult, you won't have any problems."

"But I do throw up a lot! I'm a queasebag! I get carsick and everything!" I exclaimed. My student shot me a look of speculative scrutiny. I had to be careful I didn't start a rumor that I was pregnant. "Can we discuss the details later, Rox? I'm in a conference, and I have to go teach in a few minutes."

I had time only to help my student parse her gerundive phrase, grab my lecture notes, load my briefcase, and touch up my lip gloss. Shame on Rox for dialing and diagnosing, for dropping a c-bomb in the middle of my workday! I'd have to summon my best professorial self and put that self on auto-pilot.

For the next two hours I would be lecturing on the nineteenth-century phenomenon of hysteria. In order to appreciate Charlotte Perkins Gilman's excellent short story "The Yellow Wallpaper," my students needed to hear about one Silas Weir Mitchell, the doctor who invented and marketed the infamous Rest Cure for women with, ahem, Lady Problems. This lecture was one of my favorites. It involved a number of juicy tidbits, ranging from adult diapers to leeches inserted into vaginas. At one point I reenacted a gentleman gynecologist giving an exam circa 1885.

Cheery and chatty, I was still in that no-man's-land between running six miles a day and invasive carcinoma. I laughed with my students, asking them for their impressions of the story. Then as I began writing their comments on the board, I stared at my fingers holding the chalk. They seemed to be moving with astonishing competence, covering the board with evenhanded phrases and dates, as if I had nothing to do with their message. My fingers seemed to be writing all by themselves. And I saw again the blue overhead at the healing service, realizing that three nights earlier I had been mocking a message that could have been directed to me personally.

- THROWS UP A LOT
- LADY PROBLEMS

My writing hand didn't hesitate even as I tardily began to process the implications of what Rox had told me. I might die. Even if I didn't die, I would look like Mr. Withers. Good-bye hair, brows, lashes. I wouldn't be able to run for two years. I would puke all through chemo. What if I lost my breasts? And what about Mitch? Mitch and I were only at the beginning. We hadn't even been dating four months. We didn't have the history, the strength, the elasticity, to deal with something this big.

It seemed pointedly on-topic as I lectured about the diseased female population of the late nineteenth century. I told my students about Mitchell's Rest Cure, explaining why privileged ladies of yesteryear were forced by their husbands and sons to take a protracted time-out for frail spells on the fainting couch. "Were these women even sick?" I asked my students. "Their doctors sure thought so. These were women who were whisked right out of their lives, from ballroom to bedpan. Did the doctors invent the illness so they could market a cure?"

Some of my students were nodding. They were agreeing with me. They were making it real. Rhoda Janzen, Lady Problems! Rhoda Janzen, Throws Up a Lot!

On the big blue screen of my mind a disembodied hand was printing letters that I found utterly strange, incomprehensible, as in the biblical story. King Belshazzar's guests couldn't read the message that appeared on the wall. They didn't know the language; they couldn't translate the words. I imagined the party suddenly quieting, an uneasy hush over the gathering, the chink of goblets set down abruptly. No matter that the writing on the wall was unfamiliar gibberish. We all know doom when we see it. Was it coincidence that I began returning to church just as I was forced into thinking about death?

I had unfinished business with God. What did I believe about God, really? For so many years I had been drifting on a gentle current of Christianity, as when in a paddleboat you get out to the middle of the lake and stop paddling. With scholarly neutrality I had always considered the possibility that Jesus was not divine at all. Maybe he was merely a good man and a dynamic Bible teacher, like Abe Wiens in college. The students all adored Abe Wiens, who, like Jesus, had used provocative parables to teach. Students would often brownbag his lectures, then stay for discussion and lunch. I would have gladly given up my loaves and fishes for Abe Wiens.

I had always believed that prayers of petition fell into two categories: personal requests that encouraged self-absorption, and sweet supplications on behalf of someone whose future was in no way affected by the prayer. I therefore thought that these prayers for other people were lovely but optional, like windchimes. Now it was time to clarify what I thought about prayer. The cancer had already spread to my lymph nodes, the body's transportation system. This meant that its movement to other parts of my body was highly likely, if not inevitable. I was receiving cards and emails from friends and well-wishers across the nation. Churches in Chile were praying for me. My retired pastor father, still an active public speaker, was unabashedly asking people to pray for me. He was leaving a trail of congregations on their knees. Strangers who knew my folks, or who knew friends of my folks, had heard about my case, and they wanted me to know that they were praying for my complete recovery. Relatives

I didn't even know I had were checking in with knit hats and prayers.

As far as I could see, there were two ways to read this situation. Either all that prayer mattered, or it didn't. And I needed to make up my mind.

THREE

Lip Balm in Gilead

Mennonites are known for their gorgeous a cappella hymns. For instance, they might take a Protestant staple, such as Thomas Ken's beautiful 1674 "Praise God from Whom All Blessings Flow," and jack it up like a doxology on steroids. My Mennonite church sang a highly embellished, tightly harmonized version to the tune of Samuel Stanley's "Dedication Anthem," so rousing it made you want to throw confetti. (Hey! Somebody should tell the Pentecostals about confetti!) The last two lines wind around intricate harmonies, repeating and folding back on themselves, close as hairpin turns:

> Praise him above, ye heavenly host,
> Praise Father, Son, and Holy Ghost!

The Holy Spirit is often called the Holy Ghost, maybe because nothing rhymes with *spirit*. In the Mennonite world the Holy Ghost appeared exclusively in Trinitarian-themed music, never solo, as he apparently did with the Pentecostals. Whether you called this entity the Holy Spirit or the Holy Ghost, I inferred that his disembodied state played an important role in the inner life of a believer. He was like an Invisible Friend. But honestly, Invisible Friends had always creeped me out a little.

All this talk of prayer and the Holy Ghost in Mitch's church was taking me straight back to my worst childhood fears, when I prayed prayers as repetitive as they were earnest. In my young Mennonite mind ghosts were classed with zombies and vampires, who were just a notch under demons and poltergeists. Here is an approximation of my Childhood Scale of Fear. Personally, I'd like to see a Childhood Scale of Fear make it into the psychology textbooks, along with Abraham Maslow's Hierarchy of Needs:

Top Ten Childhood Fears

in Descending Order, from Most to Least Scary

1. Demons and poltergeists; Linda Blair; Lord of the Flies; Beelzebub

2. Ghosts; zombies; vampires; Houdini séances; channeling of dead people

3. Weird Sisters (How did I get hold of *Macbeth* at the tender age of seven?)

4. Goblins; orcs; sharks; Jules Verne; denizens of below-surface kingdoms

5. Cranky fairies; leprechauns; "odd little men"; supernatural mischief makers

6. Nessie, the Loch Ness Monster; Yeti; civets; she-bears; the Sasquatch

7. Serial killers; rapists; unmarked white vans

8. Armageddon; the Four Horsemen of the Apocalypse; the Antichrist

9. A volcano in the middle of the circle drive

10. Math

For a couple of years when I was growing up we lived in the venerable Gow estate, a derelict mansion for which my parents paid $100 a month, utilities included. The mansion, built in 1890, had a long winding dirt driveway lined with magnificent old magnolias. I called my mother to ask if the Gow estate had indeed been a mansion, or if it had seemed big only because I was small.

"Oh no!" Mom said. "It *was* a mansion. Our bedroom was twenty-seven feet long! But it was falling apart. That's why they let us have it so cheap. We had to go in with shovels to get the dog poop out."

"Dog poop? Why was there dog poop?"

"Hippies brought in their dogs. They were doing drugs in there."

"The hippies or the dogs?"

"Secondhand smoke makes animals behave erratically," said my mother. "There was poop *everywhere*, in big piles."

I liked the thought of many friendly dogs pooping up a storm in a marijuana frenzy. Peace out, my brother! Maybe afterward they and their owners would be in the mood for some marshmallow Easter Peeps.

Mom told me that my father was interim pastor of a nearby church at that time, and the congregants had shown up on a series of Saturdays to help get the place in shape. They painted, they shoveled, they scrubbed. Janice Franz arrived with a kerchief, industrial gloves, and a bucket of toxic sprays. She single-handedly tackled an ancient gas oven crusted with the grime of decades. Nonny Pauls got up on a ladder and cleared out eighty years of cobwebs from the fourteen-foot ceilings. Dana Reimer and my mother took down the threadbare brocade drapes of indeterminate color—which, come to think of it, probably belonged in a museum—and Dana helped my mother dye them in a donated washing machine. These church folk rolled up their sleeves and really went for it. Mom said the entire adult Sunday School class showed up with typical Mennonite grit. Dog poop, puh-lease! Heave-ho, hippie porn! Begone, rodent colony living in the vent!

Beautiful and gloomy, the mansion would have made any child's imagination stutter. I was troubled by the weird-shaped closets, and by the maid's suite, painted a menacing shade somewhere between ochre and mauve. High on a prodigious foundation, the old floors rolled and sighed. My sister, Hannah, and I shared a terrifyingly large room, octagonal, with a fireplace. No overhead light brightened the distant ceiling, so even in the mellow light of late afternoon, the dark began to press down on us. Cloudy umber wall sconces cast long shadows, like skinny arms on the reach. The house was situated next to a citrus orchard, and we sometimes heard the restless tossing of branches, the crunch of leaves as some animal passed.

The bathroom adjoining our bedroom spooked us silly. A

high ceiling seemed grotesque in a bathroom, as if your most intimate naked activities were open and watched. Who knew how many people had reclined in the old claw-foot tub—who knew how many people had *died* in it?

I know, I know. This would seem a heavenly bathroom to us today, but imagine it as experienced by Mennonite children in sweaty flannel nighties. Rich crimson paper covered the walls. Cold octagonal floor tiles raised the hair on the back of my neck. And the toilet-paper dispenser was six feet (really!) above the floor, far above my reach when seated on the toilet. Even when I stood up, I needed a stool to reach it. I thought a lot about this toilet-paper dispenser. Who or what made the former owners place it so high above the toilet? *How were they going to the bathroom?* It all seemed unnatural, like a reverse Holy of Holies, a secret chamber for devils and demons. Sometimes I'd wake up Hannah and take her to the bathroom with me as a talisman against evil.

What's more, it was clear that there were two Otherkin living in our bedroom fireplace and closet, neither of them happy with our presence in the house. The only way to fall asleep was to immerse yourself in wholesome Laura Ingalls Wilder books. When your eyes glazed over, you'd pinch them shut and imagine fresh grasses on a wide-open prairie.

Sometimes even Laura, cheerful Half-Pint Laura, couldn't dispel the nocturnal unease. Then I'd sprint through the hall to our parents' long bedroom. This room was less scary, hosting a hive of friendly bees athrob in a fireplace papered over with old-fashioned scrolled wallpaper. Ghosty drips of honey sometimes appeared at the ceiling and meandered slowly down the wall. Meandering honey, however, was not a problem when our mother allowed us to climb into bed with her and Dad. I'd fall asleep with my mother's arm around me, her heartbeat steadying mine.

One night I awoke, instantly alert, called out of sleep by an unidentifiable sound. It came again, a footstep, a heavy pressing, as of a presence in the hall. My heart pounded. Something was out there. The door to the adjoining bathroom had been sealed off, and I would have to risk the hall if I wanted to pee. And all of a sudden I *had* to pee. My eyes, adjusting now to the hostile dark, made out the open maw of the fireplace, in which a clammy coldness was gathering. My sister was a small slumbering lump under her blankets. *Jesus*, I prayed, *Jesus, Jesus, Jesus! Make this thing go away!*

Something stirring now in the fireplace, something shagged with stink and cold. Its claws clicked on the marble. *Jesus, help me!* I lay unconsoled in the dark, until I could no longer hold it.

"Hannah!" I whispered urgently. "Hannah!"

Hannah rolled over in her single bed. Her pale curtain of hair fell away from her face. In the moonlight her hair looked otherworldly, silver as a spiderweb. It was not her fault she looked like a Child of the Corn.

"Hannah!"

I had crept out of the shabby mahogany double bed and was sitting on the edge of her mattress, sweating profusely as the cold from the fireplace began creeping up my back. Behind me the Otherkin was sitting on terrible haunches, rocking back and forth on its heels.

I shook Hannah's shoulder until she opened her eyes. She

smiled at me with the goodwill of a tractable four-year-old. But the smile revealed two pointy eyeteeth. My hand sprang back as if bitten. The thing I loved best in all the earth, this pretty fairy sister, had become a vampire!

Under circumstances like those, I think we can all agree that it is better to return to your tall monstrous bed and pee your sheets than to take your tiny vampire sister by the hand and lead her past a shuddersome entity to a bathroom in whose tub many corpses have lain.

Although I am proud to report that I no longer pee my sheets, I'm obviously still experiencing inquiry about supernatural entities. Are we not often the same people at forty-eight that we are at eight? Do we not make the same desperate petitions? Help us, we cry, make this thing, this cancer, go away! Help us, O God, for the things we love best would like to suck the life right out of us! On our very hearths lurk dark things that we try to ignore: vampires, spirits, ghosts, a long history of anxious credulity.

I never really doubted the existence of God. But I placed it like a pea under my stack of ruined mattresses. Thus I covered credulity with erudition and gentlemanly skepticism. This entailed learning the polyphony of academic doublespeak, the jargon of theory, the nitpickiness of footnotes. And, all things considered, this was an easier project than running the gauntlet to the haunted bathroom. I would rather get a PhD than stand to reach for toilet paper. Though some readers might emphasize the similarities between the two activities.

A couple of weeks ago I had lunch with a friend who did her dissertation on folkloric literature. Rosina told me that in grad school she had studied with a professor who had posited an unusual interpretation of the *mare* phenomenon. *Mare*, etymologically linked to our word *nightmare*, is the feeling that a demonic entity is sitting on your chest, riding you. You are paralyzed into speechlessness. Cultures from all over the world have reported this phenomenon. It's related, for instance, to the Newfoundland myth of Old Hag—she who leaves her own body to sit on a sleeper's ribs and harass him into gasping for speech.

This professor, a redoubtable scholar in the field, called on the idea of Occam's razor, in Latin called the *lex parsimoniae*, the law of parsimony. What if, all things being equal, the right answer is the simplest answer? What if *mare* feels like a demon on your chest because, get this, there's *actually* a demon on your chest? When Rosina repeated her professor's hypothesis, gooseflesh lifted on my arms. I changed the subject: "Let's split a dessert!" This is always a safe move, as everybody knows that demons don't go with crème brûlée.

But at age eight, whenever I tried to ask questions about the presence of evil, or demons, or the biblical Witch of Endor, my mother would shake her head and murmur, "There are powers and principalities," and change the subject. My father took a stricter approach. His voice deepened, as if buttoning up a preacherly suit jacket: "Followers of Christ want to leave those things alone."

He meant we should refrain not just from experimenting with the occult, but from even thinking about it. This was very hard to do in an era when church youth groups were aflame with stories about chatty spirits and backmasking and celestial visitations. Did you know that in the 1970s angels dressed like hitchhikers? They'd get into your van/Buick Le Sabre, ride for ten miles, and suddenly declaim "The Lord is coming soon!" Then they would vanish in the twinkling of an eye, while the car was still going. Everybody knew somebody who knew somebody to whom this had happened.

Which is all to say: Mennonites didn't really specialize in spirits, neither the Bad Guy nor the Good Guy. In our Mennonite church of origin nobody prayed to the Spirit. Nobody swayed to the Spirit. Nobody felt the presence of the Spirit as a light breeze or a gust of wind. And above all, nobody spoke in tongues. Mitch said if I kept coming to church, I'd eventually hear people speaking in tongues.

Mitch and I were seriously into each other. Everything about his manner said, "I want you to keep coming with me to church, and to the grocery store, and the drugstore, and even my dad's Widows & Widowers dinner at Beachwood Inn, which serves green beans from a can." The day that I got the cancer diagnosis I dropped by Mitch's workplace. Although it was late, I thought I should deliver the bad news right away. He deserved to be told straight-up that I didn't expect him to stick around. Who would?

In the dark parking lot I skirted hulking trailers and semis, picking my way up a crowded ramp to a massive steel door. I had never been inside a warehouse before. It was dark and cavernous. In the distance a guy in a Carhartt jacket was heaving things onto a hi-lo. "Excuse me!" I shouted. "I'm looking for Mitch."

"Butch?"

"Mitch!"

The man waved and took out his phone. In the shadowy entrance I waited for a long time, impatient now that I had decided to break it off fast and clean.

Suddenly Mitch was standing in front of me, big and oily in his coveralls. I sneezed three times, very fast.

"I been sweepin'," he said. "You got the results?"

"It's cancer and it's bad." I sneezed several more times, as if for emphasis. "A tumor at least three inches long, maybe more. They need to do some more tests. I think we should break up."

"No."

"Okay, you need to listen, really listen, to what I'm going to say. I've talked to Rox twice and checked the stats. There's a strong likelihood that I won't make it. The tumor is so large it's inoperable. You can't plunge a new relationship into this sort of trauma and expect it to survive. I say we call it quits before it gets ugly."

He freely spread his dirty hand on the top of my head, like a hat. "But it ain't your right to make that choice for me. This is my choice, sugar. I'm the right man for this."

"How can you possibly know that?"

"I know what I know."

He got up in my space then, schmutz on my nice charcoal jacket.

Arms locked around his neck, I said, "Okay. But you have my permission to bail at any time."

He chuckled. "Ain't nobody gonna bail. You watch and see what the Lord's gonna do."

∽

My oncologist, who has an excellent sense of humor, agreed to write me a prescription for a "cranial prosthesis." I therefore embarked on a wig-shopping spree that would have given pause to Dolly Parton. All four of the wig shops in Grand Rapids are owned by Korean women who forbid photographs. So Mitch whipped out the camera while my sister distracted the ladies with pressing questions about skull caps. I've got to hand it to my sister for creating a variety of plausible scenarios that explained why I was trying on wigs in every shade, from Stripper Red to Silver Fox, and in every shape, from Crouching Tiger to Economy Igloo. Thanks to Mitch's alert photography, this stage of my cancer journey was very well documented.

The Midwest has its style challenges, so I finally ordered a wig online. You're supposed to send in a swatch of your own hair for an exact match. Over the years my natural blond had darkened to a shade that I would describe as "Bunny on the Lawn." With the help of expensive highlights I made my peace with this shade. But I'd rather have my sister's totally natural shade, which we might call "Pale Ethereal Moonbeam." I was all set to send in a swatch of cosmetically enhanced Bunny on the Lawn, mixed with Hannah's Pale Ethereal Moonbeam, when my mother remembered two braids she had thoughtfully preserved when I was three years old.

"Aaron was playing cowboys and Indians," she said reminiscently. "He snuck up behind you to scalp you, and he cut off your braids."

"Was I the cowboy?"

"No, you were shelling peas. I saved the braids because they were such a pretty pale blond. They're in the garage at home. I'll send them to you. You can use them as the color swatch for your cancer wig."

While the Jessica was an excellent match for my junior-mint braids, it turned out that I looked okay without hair. Eventually I decided to go around bald, like a Chihuahua. The Jessica looked convincingly real with a beret, but who wants to wear a beret every single day? In the first couple of weeks of chemo, however, I did wear the Jessica-beret combo daily because I wanted to sidestep pitying looks from strangers. One Sunday morning I went as usual to church with Mitch. My cream-colored angora beret covered the Jessica's hairline, and my locks looked newly highlighted; nobody would have guessed that I was bald as a knob underneath. My eyebrows and lashes stayed with me a full two months after I lost my head hair. In other words, on this Sunday, I still looked fine, fit from years of running. Over-the-knee shearling boots gave me some sassy Sherpa *je ne sais quoi*. I thought I was looking pretty good for a doomed cancer babe.

Nobody at Mitch's church knew about my condition or my chemo anyway. At that point I had been attending only a couple of months and didn't know very many people. My pattern was to sprint out the door as soon as church was dismissed. I was terrified that a well-meaning believer would buttonhole me, hand me a tract, and inquire whether I'd enjoy a basket of muffins and a nice chat about my status as an unrepentant sinner. Making social connections with the churchgoers was something I was not ready to do. When they nodded and smiled at me, my answering nod said, "Muffins—oh no you don't!"

Immediately after the service, a burly midlife man approached us and introduced himself as Elder Joe. I had never seen him before. He was holding a wee tin of something that looked like lip balm. We shook hands.

Elder Joe said, "I don't know what your condition is, Rhoda, but last Wednesday it was suddenly heavy on my heart to pray for you. This feeling was really heavy, and it became more pronounced throughout the week. I believe the Holy Spirit wants me to tell you something."

Messages from the spirit world! "What is it?" I said, nervous.

"Last year a woman who goes to this church was healed of stage-four cancer. Mitch knows her—"

Mitch nodded. "That's right. Anita Cruz."

"—and this healing happened right after we prayed over her at the altar. She had breast cancer that had metastasized to her lungs, and her doctors were referring her to hospice."

I looked at Mitch as if to say, "Did you set this thing up?" He silently shook his head.

Elder Joe went on, "I've been praying for you since Wednesday. I believe you have some illness, maybe breast cancer, even though you look to be in full health. What I would like to do is pray over you at the altar, and anoint you with oil." He indicated the little tin that looked like lip balm.

While I was dumbly following him to the pulpit at the front of the church, another elder flagged us down. This was a woman I recognized, Elder Justine. We had never been formally introduced, but we had smiled at each other once or twice, and I respected the way she always seemed to go out of her way to include women in the services. For example, if there was an ordination of a pastoral couple, and if the pastor was focusing exclusively on the man, Elder Justine would jump in and launch a long prayer for the wife of this man. She always called women by their first names, too—never Mrs. This and Mrs. That. She was the only woman I had seen speaking during the service.

"Excuse me," Elder Justine said, hurrying up to us as we were making our way to the front of the church. "I don't even know your name, but I have a message for you."

Now I was flat-out freaked.

"This morning when I was taking off my coat, I saw you coming in, and suddenly I heard a voice, a real voice, saying in my ear, *'Tell her I have her back.'*"

"Oh!" I said, simultaneously creeped out and appalled.

Justine took my arm. I was about a foot taller than she, and she was standing very close to me, face pressed into my shoulder. "This is a message from the Spirit," she said, eyes strangely intense. *'I have your back.'*"

And suddenly I felt something, something that passed between me and this woman, something that jumped from her to me. It was light, it was electric, it made my heart race. Tears sprang into my eyes—I, who am not usually a crier!

But if there was a real Spirit, why hadn't he told me the message himself?

I now know the answer to this question. Who would try to talk to somebody who is obviously not listening?

I didn't want a message from the Holy Spirit delivered through a woman I didn't know. What I wanted was the direct, unmistakable God of ancient biblical times, the Spirit who appeared smack in front of Moses in a burning bush, with a directive to Moses, for Moses, about Moses. A burning bush you couldn't argue with. But I was too freaked out to quibble, and anyway, Elder Joe was already praying and touching my forehead with what I'm still convinced was lip balm. As he prayed, Justine laid her hands on my shoulders and began speaking in tongues, a strange quiet rushing sound, a cross between a pigeon cote and a fast-running brook. Syllables rolled all around me like pearls from a broken string, scattering beyond sense.

I had never heard anyone speak in tongues. I had always assumed that glossolalia was an expression of unfiltered inner gibberish. But in that moment I wondered if it couldn't be both gibberish *and* praise language—an edifying wall of sound that lifted the worshipper to a place beyond understanding.

Even if those gorgeous waves of foreign syllables had come rolling out of my own mouth, I still would have tried to understand the experience as a foreign language. Indeed, if Rosetta Stone offered a course in Holy Ghost for Beginners, I'd have ordered levels 1–5 to work on my verbs. While one part of my mind was listening intently to Justine, trying to make sense of the beautiful rushing momentum, my spirit relaxed within me, as it does when I'm in a country whose language I don't speak. In such a circumstance you can't be expected to understand the effluvium of sounds. You just look around and go, "Glad I'm here."

On the way out I clutched Mitch's arm, profoundly unsettled.

"Did you tell anyone at this church I have cancer?" I demanded.

"No, honey. Not my business to do that."

"Oh! Why do I feel so WEIRD?"

He looked at me with compassion. "That's the Holy Spirit. When Elder Joe started prayin over you, I felt a breeze movin over my chest. Didn't you feel it?"

"No," I said. "Maybe that was me, gasping in surprise."

I didn't tell him what I knew to be true. This experience had changed something for me. I had no words to explain the jolt I had received. It was not logical. Indeed, the entire experience was so bizarre that I saw at once I would be unable to reason it out. Thinking was out. If I began thinking about this, about the meaning of Justine's fierce voice and strange eyes, I would end up arriving where I always arrived, at the threshold I could never quite bring myself to cross. I was already beginning to excuse and diminish the experience. "Well, of *course* spiritual experiences can seem real—that's why people believe in them!"

But the syllables, the pearls, the tears! Did I even need to understand prayer? Why not sit back with the lip balm on my head, and just believe?

FOUR

⤜

Hot Rock

S ome sisters only pretend to like each other. When they speak of each other, their lips thin like pressed leaves and their tone takes on a crunchy sugar coating. "My sister? Well, her choices aren't my choices, but she's still my sister. Of course I love her." This translates as "That wench regifted me some heinous zebra hand towels." My sister Hannah and I have always marveled at our genuine compatibility and our shared taste. Luckily we do not attack one another with zebra hand towels. Before I was diagnosed with cancer, we took turns visiting each other, interpreting the long plane ride as a chance to read some frivolous self-help.

One day when she had flown in from the West Coast, we were lounging with our respective books on my deck. We came across an astonishing claim in the work of Wayne Dyer. Up until that moment Dyer had been making rather grandiloquent sense. He narrated a story about—what else?—parenting. His teenager, Sands, favored hardcore music with lyrics about death and destruction. I don't know why adolescents everywhere cotton to violent lyrical images involving bitches and pimps, but it is so. "Smack my bitch up!" Easy listening at its finest.

Dyer was claiming that all inanimate objects have energy vibrations that calibrate high (positive energy) or low (negative energy). He asked his son to perform a simple test. Sands would hold up an organic life form, say a banana, with his arm stretched out horizontally as far as he could reach. Then using one hand only, Dyer senior would try to press his son's banana hand down toward the floor. Because the banana vibrated with positive energy, the son's hand would easily resist the attempt to push it down. They tried it. Indeed, said Dyer, the banana remained level. Altogether it was a high and mighty banana. But when Sands held out his low-energy CD with the violent lyrics, the arm descended as of its own accord, having been weakened by the negative vibrations of an inanimate object.

"Oh wow," said Hannah, as soon as I had read this out loud. "That's some craaaaazy talk! Do you have a banana?"

"Gross. How about a wholesome, life-affirming pink grapefruit?"

"Perfect."

We went inside and procured a grapefruit. Because I didn't yet own an iPod, I jumped up to find a CD that was sufficiently satanic. "I can't find anything that augurs a malevolent or surly attitude," I said over my shoulder from the wall of CDs.

"Well, there's got to be something dark and angry on that wall, for heaven's sake."

None of my CDs seemed particularly satanic, so we settled on the soundtrack for the movie *Trainspotting*, a 1996 film about disaffected teens addicted to heroin. "I wouldn't describe this music as negative," I said cautiously. "But it does feature a song by Iggy Pop. Iggy Pop once masturbated onstage and then hid in the trunk of his car when the police came to arrest him for indecent exposure."

"Why would you masturbate onstage?" Hannah asked, studying the CD jacket.

"Maybe you get carried away in a kind of Dionysian performance frenzy. It's funnier that he hid in the trunk of his car."

Hannah seemed willing to consider Iggy as a semi-satanic substitute. "Sure, okay. Nobody would say that Iggy Pop is life-affirming. Look at his titles. *Zombie Birdhouse, Skull Ring, Beat 'em Up—*"

"Perfect!"

"Let's do it. Press down on my hand."

The grapefruit in my sister's hand remained poised, vibrating busily with unseen spiritual benefits.

"Now Iggy."

I pressed her hand again, exerting the same amount of force. Down went the hand.

"Stop it," I said. "Do it right."

"I *did*! Oh my God, this must mean that Iggy Pop is the devil!"

We freshened our drinks, giggling.

"Now me," I said. I extended the grapefruit, steady as Gibraltar. Hannah's hand didn't budge it. But when she pressed down on Iggy Pop, my arm dipped down helplessly. We were enthralled with the idea that inanimate objects might offer up commentary on their moral worth—this was better than a fortune cookie! "What else can we try it with?"

"Bust out those silicone butt pads!"

My flat derriere is a joke in my circle of family and friends. The rear view looks not unlike the white cliffs of Dover. Curvy up front, I've never needed to wear a padded bra. Therefore padded undergarments for the rear never registered on my lingerie radar. In fact it had never even occurred to me that there were women out there who were peacefully faking booty. But my girlfriend Theresa, having heard me vent for a full decade on the verticality of my backside, had sent me a pair of panties into which one could tuck two accompanying silicone butt pads.

The padded panties yielded a high, tight, subtle curve. Impressive, I thought in surprise, standing in front of the mirror in my closet. But imagine if a guy was really into your rear topography and then it turned out that the hinterland was all drama? Also, wasn't a padded panty significantly sadder than a padded bra? A padded panty seemed desperate and needy, whereas a padded bra was an expression of reasonable hyperbole, as when an acquaintance says, "How are you?" and you say, "Fantastic!"

Theresa told me I had to wear the padded panty in public at least once and then report back to her. I opted for a pair of snug jeans on my day of booty-enhanced errands. And I am sorry to report that the padded panty did make a marked difference in how men looked at me. The stunt butt must have been freakishly compelling, because its eerie power trumped the twin competing factors of middle age and a T-shirt that said

BANANA SPLIT INFINITIVE

A forty-five-year-old woman in a grammar T-shirt, heaping her shopping cart with faro, chickpeas, and personal watermelons, does not ordinarily attract overtures from male shoppers. However, that afternoon I received two overtures. I think women have seriously underestimated the social networking possibilities of grocery stores. Singles websites—who needs 'em? Just grab your padded panties and head for the radicchio!

My day was spooling along as normal until I went to the bathroom at Target. When I stood up to flush, one of the butt pads jumped out of its pouch and hit the floor, gleaming on the gray tile like a gelatinous chicken cutlet. I snatched it up, horrified, wondering if the woman in the next stall had seen it. Finally she departed. It was then and there that I made a decision. If I was going to be bombing the floor with silicone cutlets, then padded panties were not the garment for me.

Hannah and I hypothesized that the cutlets, unlike the life-affirming grapefruit, would dip down when pressed. The cutlets represented fakery, dishonesty, the deliberately misleading promises of artifice. O Cutlet! When old age shall this generation waste, thou shalt remain! We figured that anything fake should vibrate with seriously limp energy.

But the cutlets remained firm and horizontal when pressed. How was it that the universe was willing to go thumbs-down on Iggy Pop, but that it would give fake butt pads a thumbs-up? Hannah's padded bra also passed muster. "Thank heavens," said Hannah. "I wasn't about to ditch my bra just because it was evil. That sucker cost eighty-five bucks."

I later recalled the cosmic endorsement of the butt pads when I understood that my breasts were goners. Soon I would be depositing a different set of silicone pads directly inside my core anatomy, a thing I thought I would never do. Clearly the occasion called for thoughtful reflection. Shouldn't fake breasts do a little more than fill out a bra, given the protracted pain of the reconstruction process? Was it too much to ask for some multitasking? I thought of the seventies television show *The Bionic Woman*. When Lindsey Wagner was coming to grips with her new bionic powers, her first realization was that *she could open a can of tuna with her thumbnail*. The director rightly filmed this event in slow motion, due to its magnificence and overall plot impact. And so here is my question: at the very least, shouldn't a replacement breast be able to open a can of tuna?

My mother pointed out that nobody was forcing me to do the reconstruction.

"Mom!" I said. "Are you suggesting that I walk around perfectly flat-chested?"

"Why not? Your Great Aunt Nettie had a mastectomy, and she went around for years in a cardigan that was flat on one side."

"She could have stuffed a sock in her bra."

"No, she just cut the cup out of her bra. She showed me. She wanted some support, but only on one side."

My oncologist's nurse sent me home with a cancer starter kit. It featured plenty of pamphlets, an advance directive, a big three-ring binder, and a canvas tote that said THE LEMMEN HOLTON CANCER PAVILION. As if I wanted to own cancer by announcing it in my wardrobe: boo.

I discarded the pamphlets and completed the form, though it was hard to choose which of my friends would inherit the shoe wardrobe and the art, Mitch being indifferent to both. At first I didn't understand why I would need a binder. ("Why, thanks, an enormous three-ring binder!") Did cancer people scrapbook? Were there to be Precious Memories? However, as soon as the onslaught of medical bills and insurance statements commenced, it became clear that one needs a three-ring binder the way an alert Ketchikan backpacker needs bear spray.

I read lots of studies about the value of positive visualization. Positive visualization may not have been the ultimate weapon of choice, but, like bear spray, it was better than nothing. One study reported that a Dr. Carl Simonton encouraged his patients to imagine their cancer cells as being eaten by a giant PAC-MAN. I got busy on Etsy and ordered some temporary tattoos in the shape of hungry, open-mouthed PAC-MEN. These I liberally applied to my breasts. First things first.

Your life, any life, can change overnight. In the core of my being I knew this, but like many people, I preferred to direct any free-floating anxiety toward more manageable worries, such as cellulite. Medical appointments were landing with random pertinacity, like shrapnel after a blast. My heart sank as my planner filled. It was beginning to look as if I wouldn't be able to finish the semester, even though the chemo wouldn't commence until December.

How could I leave my students in the lurch midsemester? Ah, how fond I was of my foolish little theory of indispensability! It was humbling to confront the truth. And the truth was: I was expendable. If I dropped dead, life would go on busily for my students and friends. No wonder people preferred to think about cellulite. Before I could even articulate my anxieties, though, my professor friends stepped up to take over my classes. My colleagues, spectacularly efficient, organized a brigade of meals, rides, books, and meditation tapes. Within twenty-four hours I was looking at a huge stockpile of supplies. Well, if I failed to have a nice cancer journey, I'd have only myself to blame. I had a stalwart boyfriend, tender girlfriends, a mother who cheated at Scrabble, and a series of handknit hats, each cuter than the last. Bring on the baldness.

I still had to finalize things with my grammar teaching assistant, Sherman, aka "The Snow Leopard." At my college, students bound for grad school study pedagogy by shadowing an actual professor. It's such a time investment that I limit myself to one trainee per semester. Sherman was a gifted student who wore a stretch terry headband low on his forehead, pulled snugly down on his shaggy bangs, like Bjorn Borg. Unlike Bjorn Borg, Sherman did not play tennis. Sherman was a creative writing major specializing in fiction. But since I didn't teach fiction, I had never worked with him except in academic English classes, where his astute analyses and laconic comments always blew away the competition. And in the three years I had known him, I had never seen him without the headband. You have to give it up for a young maverick who holds to his dream of wearing a Bjorn Borg headband.

I had to tell Sherman that I would be unable to finish out the semester with him. We were walking together to what would be my last class. Because my arm was sore from exploratory surgery, Sherman was carrying my briefcase. It was a beautiful stainless-steel Halliburton, very professional. Sherman was far too shaggy and young to be carrying this urban spy briefcase. Polite, he was waiting for me to say something.

"Hey," I began. "I have cancer."

"Bummer."

"This is going to be my last class. There's a volley of tests before I start chemo, so Professor Vissers will be taking over the grammar class."

"I know Carla," he said. "She's cool. What about next semester?"

I shook my head. "I'm taking the semester off." I didn't know how much I should say to a student, so I added, "It's not just the chemo. There are a couple of bigger surgeries coming up."

We were picking our way across a snowy street. Sherman looked both ways for traffic and remarked, as if to a general audience, "I wonder if you can feel the breast when it's gone, the way amputees feel their missing leg."

I liked this line of speculation. "It's called phantom limb pain."

"Maybe you can write an essay called 'The Phantom Tit,'" he suggested. "I know that if I were browsing the journals in a library I would pick up an essay called 'The Phantom Tit.'"

"I'll dedicate it to you," I promised.

"It could be sort of a ghost story," he went on. "Like Edith Wharton's 'The Eyes.' The protagonist is visited in the night by a big ghostly tit that has some kind of troubling message."

"Like a Stephen King screenplay?"

"No," said Sherman. "I'm not saying it's a *malevolent* tit. It's not a *Carrie* tit. It just has something to say. It wants to be heard."

"Okay," I said, "as long as it doesn't hide under the bed or usher in an envoy of fellow amputations from a nearby burial ground."

"I don't think so," said Sherman, frowning. "I think this tit says, 'I come in peace.' It's an approachable tit."

"In that case, I gladly acknowledge it as my new invisible friend. Am I the only one who can see it?"

"You begin to question your sanity."

"Forgive me for introducing a practical concern," I said. "But the tit in question is alive, attached to my chest wall even as we speak. Why doesn't it communicate its message right now? It has until May 10 to speak up."

The Snow Leopard stopped dead in his tracks, not missing a beat. He looked at me keenly. "Maybe it already has. Maybe *you're not listening*!"

My family and friends on the West Coast had a hard time getting their minds around my diagnosis. You know how in every family there's the Smart One and the Beautiful One and the Successful One? In our family I was the One Who Ate Bok Choy. Cancer seemed the wrong disease, given my healthy lifestyle. It took us a collective minute to regroup. But as soon as my mother and sister understood what lay ahead, they launched a plan of action. Hannah would fly out immediately, leaving her husband and daughter for seven weeks; she would support me through the first battery of procedures and the port installation. My mother would arrive later, to cheer me through the first half of chemo. Then my mother would return four months later, when I would theoretically be well enough for a double mastectomy. Meanwhile we would play Scrabble. Turns out that a confrontation with mortality does not make you lose interest in Scrabble, so we planned a nice overlap of three weeks when all three of us would be together.

How licensed mammographers could have missed a tumor the size of a baseball during sixteen years of regular mammograms is puzzling, but I think I've got it figured out. When my brother Aaron and I were kids, we often managed the tedium of long-winded sermons by playing a game with the maps in the back of my white leather Bible. We would whisper unfamiliar place-names to each other, and then time how long it took the other to locate the obscure city or town. Even at nine years, Aaron considered himself Lord of Geography. Khan Yenis! Shechem! Tel Zit! I quickly realized that the only way to take him down was to whisper the name of a country so colossal, so *obvious*, that it was hidden in plain sight, spelled out in huge letters across the map:

C H A D

Maybe the mammographers were so busy looking for tiny towns that they just didn't see the enormous Chad of a tumor in front of their very noses, sprawling across the Sahara of my chest.

After receiving confirmation that the tumor was indeed huge, my sister and I went shopping, since we were in Grand Rapids anyway. At the Gap I found a pair of really long pants, pants that were mutantly and enchantingly long, so long that I could wear my highest heels with them. On sale for $12.99! On the one hand, I had an epic invasive tumor; on the other, there were the pants. Score.

In subsequent days, I was treated to a delectable variety of tests, CAT scans and MRIs, many of which involved swallowing a berry-flavored radioactive beverage. Somewhere sixteen executives in a boardroom must have had this conversation:

CHAIRPERSON, *popping several antacids.* Team, we've got a radioactive product that tastes so bad it triggers vomiting on contact. Any suggestions?

VISIONARY. Boss, what if we flavor it with the taste of— stay with me now—artificial *berries?*

TEAM, *scattered applause, whistles.* You go, Einstein!

CHAIRPERSON. By gum, you're a genius! That's inspired! *Berries!*

At least now I would be able to introduce my sister to my new boyfriend. Given my track record in romance, I was anxious to hear Hannah's opinion of Mitch. And I didn't just want to *get* Hannah's advice. I wanted to *take* it. Her counsel was the best I knew. In her romantic life she had chosen wisely, and she knew me better than anyone alive.

In the last two years I had reassessed the role of counsel in my life. In the past I had often asked my girlfriends Carla and Julie for advice, particularly over cocktails at Butch's. But I had solicited their counsel mainly in order to while away a pleasurable happy hour. By this I mean that I reserved the right to go on doing whatever I had been doing in the first place. In fact I rarely changed my behavior. Carla, Julie, and I didn't want to *change* each other. We wanted to love each other and eat yummy little pretzels with honey mustard.

Now, however, I was serious about taking wise counsel. The plan was to introduce Mitch and Hannah over a nice, low-key, left-breast, MRI-assisted biopsy. Early in the morning, before the roads had been plowed, Mitch showed up for the long drive to the hospital. He presented us with a tray of gas-station coffee. My sister, a soignée foodie, accepted her bad coffee with thanks. I couldn't tell if she was thinking, "Ah, what a dear and thoughtful gesture!" or "Ah, a cloying hazelnut additive in this fake creamer!"

At the hospital Hannah and Mitch settled into the waiting room. No spark of conviviality had leaped up between them. I wondered what Mitch and Hannah would find to talk about during my procedure. As the nurse escorted me into the changing room, I looked back over my shoulder. A pale curtain of hair had swung forward across my sister's face, so I couldn't see her expression. But her listening posture signaled that a serious conversation had already commenced. Her beautiful legs were crossed, her high-heeled boots the last word in sable elegance. Beside her Mitch was leaning forward in his thick flannel shirt, hands on his knees, speaking with great deliberation. I waved. They didn't see me.

Later Hannah reported that Mitch had plunged in, as if small talk were a frippery for tea parties. He had turned to her and announced, "Someday I hope to marry your sister, but you should know straight from me that for fifteen years I was an alcoholic until the Lord set me free."

"Hah," I said. "Did he tell you about the boozy incident with the chainsaw?"

"Yup."

"Did he tell you he cheated on his ex-wife?"

"With the lady truck driver."

"Did he tell you about the Molotov cocktail at Baker Furniture?"

"No. But he did indicate a youth of juvenile delinquency."

"One of his buddies was found dead in the state park," I said, holding an ice pack to my left breast. "He was shot in the head execution-style, like in a bad movie."

"He didn't tell me that," said Hannah. "But he did mention that he was quite the entrepreneur in the field of recreational drugs."

"At any point in the briefing did he use the word *ganjah*?"

She clinked my teacup with hers.

"Did he tell you his credit score?"

Hannah laughed so hard she had to set her cup down. "Really? His credit score?"

I nodded. "On the fourth date. He had it all printed out in a little folder and everything. When he walked me to the door, he handed me the folder and said, 'I want you to look at this. It ain't bad. But it's real important to me that you read it.' So naturally I was expecting a poem about how he had turned over a new leaf. But it was a full-blown, hands-on, nine-page credit report."

That night Hannah brought me a fistful of pills, having organized my many new prescriptions into a phalanx of clearly labeled bottles. I swallowed obediently, still a bit woozy from the last dose. "Do you need anything?" she asked as I lay back in bed.

"I'm not an invalid," I said indignantly. "It's only a little cancer."

"It's only a *big* cancer."

"Size doesn't matter," I said. "I'll be up and running again before you know it."

She turned out my light and stood silhouetted in the doorway. "Rhoda."

"Yeah?"

"Mitch is the real thing. Better hang on to him."

When Hannah and I went to pick up my mother at the airport, she hugged us, smiling and teary-eyed. Mom had just lost another of her brothers to cancer, and she was feeling weepy as she hugged her freshly diagnosed daughter. Hannah and I shared a smile above Mom's head. We knew her tears wouldn't last long. You can check your watch: three, two, one, now! She blew her nose, looked around, and pointed to one of those vending machines that rent films. "Let's have a nice glass of milk," she said.

"Okay," I said. "But we'll have to stop somewhere on the way home."

She pointed again to the movie kiosk. "No, let's just have some here."

Hannah and I looked at each other, then shrugged. We examined the kiosk.

Mom was pointing to an advertisement for a film in which Sean Penn plays the gay activist Harvey Milk.

My mother did desire to swing by the store on the way home, so even though it was snowing hard, I pulled into one of those supersized chain stores that have everything from fennel to furniture. I figured she just wanted to make sure I had enough fruits and vegetables. She told me to wait in the car, and she took my sister in with her. They came back not with groceries, but a huge Yamaha keyboard. "I thought you would want to practice playing hymns while you have cancer," my mother said brightly. "I brought you a *Gesangbuch*."

I grew up in a German-speaking community. While I have not sung German hymns for many a decade, I think we can all agree that a German hymnbook is a thoughtful, relevant gift for those in chemotherapy.

I play piano slowly and clumsily, by sight, not by ear. I've never even taken lessons, unless you count two ill-fated Saturday mornings when I was eight. Once a boyfriend gave me a harmonica, but he complained that I kept holding it like a corn on the cob. My musical training is therefore undistinguished. But what says, "Cancer schmancer!" better than a Yamaha keyboard? That very night my mother set the thing up, watched the directional video, and treated us to "We Three Kings of Orient Are." With a techno beat.

I was on fire with my Yamaha keyboard. Back away, everybody! Can't touch this! Who's gettin' down to "Gott ist die Liebe" with a funkedelic groove interspersed with traffic noises and/or fireworks? Consider, if you will, the classic hymn "Nun danket alle Gott" played above the sound of World War I artillery fire. During the chorus you can bring in a veritable pot-pourri of aural pleasures: a bleating lamb, a cuckoo clock, or an inexplicable sound the Yamaha folks describe as "goblins." It turns out that playing bad keyboard is something you can do queasy or well, early or late! It helps if you sing in German at the top of your lungs.

On New Year's Eve, the night after Mitch shaved my head, I was demonstrating how one might spice up the classic German Christmas carol "O Tannenbaum" with a background track of helicopter noise, as in *Apocalypse Now*. I sang all three verses, adding gunshots, telephones, and goblins as needed. When it was over, I pressed the "applause" button and took a deep bow.

Mitch clapped and rose to answer me in kind, as at the opera. He didn't play an instrument, but he sang with gusto in a booming semimusical bass, hitting the notes maybe 70 percent of the time. Staying with the tune of "O Tannenbaum," he made up the words as he went along. I loved it when he did this, though whenever I tried to harmonize with him, he abandoned the melody and wandered off into a tuneless no-man's-land somewhere between the Grand Ole Opry and a Lynyrd Skynyrd concert:

O chemo girl, O chemo girl,
your head is bald and tiny.
I don't know why your head's so small
You look like Maddy's Barbie doll
O chemo girl, O chemo girl,
your head is bald and tiny.

I had purchased a snug little beanie in the boys' section at Marshall's. This I now removed and set smartly atop Mitch's own huge head. The beanie was too small to stretch, so I left it sitting there like a wee biscuit while I ran to get my camera.

"Let's get some pictures of that gorgeous sunset over the lake," my mother said after she had tractably photographed Mitch's and my matching bald heads. "Don't the branches look beyoootiful under the ice? The icicles remind me of the time my dad loaded us into the stone boat for the Christmas concert at the schoolhouse."

We waited expectantly. My mother's stories could take any direction at all.

"It was terribly cold, just like tonight, so my dad heated up a big rock on the coal stove. He harnessed up the horses and—"

"He harnessed a boat to his horses?" Mitch interrupted.

"A stone boat. It was like a glorified sled, a raft with rudders. It had a bench but no sides. So he put the hot rock by the bench and shouted for us to come. Trude, Hilde, Anya, and I ran out in our mittens and coats. Then Dad threw a horse blanket over us."

"He covered your heads up with a horse blanket?" I asked.

"The wind was sharp," she explained. "We couldn't see a thing. But it wasn't too bad because we were huddled around the rock. Meanwhile it was so cold that the stone boat froze into the snow. Dad said 'Giddyap!' to the horses. They tried to go, but we were stuck. He shouted 'Giddyap!' again, and this time the horses jerked the stone boat forward so hard that the bench flew off and we were all thrown into the snow. I wish we had a picture of *that*!"

I did too—little Loewens tumbling down the snowbank, dresses up, legs akimbo, panties made of flour sacks, the helpless giggles.

"What a good dad he was," she said. "Trying to make us comfortable for a mile-long trip."

Ah, hot rocks and horse blankets over the head—good times, good times. It would have been easy to tell this story with a different punch line, for instance, *Can you believe what a Dummkopf Opa was, not even bothering to secure the bench?* But my mother, now playing sudoku by the fire, wasn't thinking about the man's sins of omission. It never would have occurred to her to stress her father's failure to secure the bench, or even the children's failure to climb back up the snowbank. Facts may wobble out of our control, but interpretation is ours to command. You get knocked off the bench. Horses jerk you around. The key is to notice that somebody loves us all.

It's no surprise that my mom is a glass-half-full kind of gal. She's not one to bear a grudge or to dredge up old hurts. But forgiveness hasn't always come easily to me. At the time my divorce went through, I thought that grudges were something that arrived ineluctably, like gnats on fruit. They came according to circumstance, and they would leave according to season. I was under the impression that grudges just *happened* to people, and that you had to carry them as long as they lasted. My readings in Eastern philosophy had left me with a stoic attitude toward all negative emotion: this too shall pass. Suck it up and wait it out.

I didn't know then that there are specific, habitual actions you can take that move you toward forgiveness. While I was open to the idea of God, I had not yet arrived at a healthy understanding of what *I* needed to do to promote my own spiritual growth. Thus in the aftermath of my divorce I just sort of sat there like a big well-dressed dummy, waiting tentatively for a magic moment from God.

But change was a-comin'. I began to use the law of displacement as demonstrated by my ninth-grade physics teacher, Mr. Wurby. Mr. Wurby showed the class that when sand is poured into a full glass of water, in goes the sand and out comes the water. This means that gratitude and grudges won't fit into the same glass. If you add gratitude, out comes the grudge.

You don't need to have amazing things to be grateful for. For a while there my life was so entirely in the crapper that I really had to reach. I found myself calling out some lame gratitudes. "Today I am happy and grateful that I have never dated a part-time stripper known as The Rumpshaker." "Today I am happy and grateful that I do not have a deadly peanut allergy." "Today I am happy and grateful that I was not born in the 1880s, when those velveteen Little Lord Fauntleroy suits were all the crack." To my surprise, even these lame gratitudes did the trick. So Mr. Wurby, if you're still alive, at this time I would like to retract my prediction that our ninth-grade activities relating to sand displacement would never yield practical results.

Like most people when they first approach God, all I wanted was help. I was hoping God might swoop in and do the work for me. He didn't do that. But he did show me how to do the work myself. One day something clicked into focus, as when you use binoculars to scan a wintery vista in which branches blur the landscape. Suddenly you lock on to a shape that under your very eyes gathers muscle and momentum—you see an enormous hawk, sitting in splendid indifference high above the shoreline. My hawk was the tardy epiphany that I had spent a lifetime blaming other people for my own stuff. The sheer force of this revelation took my breath away. It changed everything. All of a sudden I saw that holding a grudge was a way *to avoid confronting my own stuff.* And so for the last two years the idea of prayer had been slowly gathering heft. At the time of my diagnosis I saw faith in God not as belief in a real external entity, but as a useful cause-and-effect strategy for managing heartbreak, anxiety, and blame.

Around nine my mother announced that she was going to bed.

"Stay up with us and see in the new year," suggested Mitch.

"I'm in the middle of a good book. You two raise a glass for me." She nodded at the club soda waiting on ice as if it were champagne.

"How do you celebrate New Year's at home these days?" I asked.

"We go to bed early, same as always. But on New Year's Day Si makes *Portzelky*, and we usually have folks over."

"No New Year's resolutions for you?" asked Mitch.

"Pshaw," said my mother. "We just say a prayer for the new year. I usually ask God for the wisdom to manage whatever the year will bring. Maybe this year I'll ask him for a nice son-in-law." She reached up to kiss Mitch's cheek and said good night.

We turned out all the lights and lounged away the hours by firelight. Outside it was breathlessly clear, the lake brittle, the sky iced with stars. Crystals shagged the pines. We cuddled under a cozy throw. Drowsy from my meds but wanting to make it to midnight, I wouldn't let myself drift off against Mitch's warmth. Instead I thoughtfully inserted my cold feet under his sweatshirt.

"You're a hot rock in the stone boat of life," I said.

"I'd rather be the horse that pulls the boat."

"Okay. I'll be the snowbank, ready to receive the cattywampus who have fallen and can't get up."

The cat jumped on to the couch and turned a couple of doglike circles before settling down to knead Mitch's stomach, exactly as if my feet had not staked a prior claim. In the silence a full-bodied purr arose like one of the sound effects on my keyboard.

"Honey, your cat likes me."

"That's because you feed him directly off your plate."

"No, it's because I stick my fingers in his ears." He demonstrated this technique. The cat was beside himself with pleasure. "I wedge 'em in there and itch 'em around where he can't scratch."

"Gross," I said. "Wash your hands before you kiss me."

In answer he shooed Lars and pressed me back onto the couch. "I'm serious," I said, holding him off with a queenly cancer card. "My immune system is low, and you don't know what kind of cooties are in his ears."

"Your bald head looks kinda blue in this light."

"I have more to say on the topic of cooties," I said.

"One minute till midnight."

We counted down the last ten seconds and kissed in spite of the threat to my immune system.

"Are we done talkin about ear mites?" he asked.

"Is there a subject you would prefer?"

He sat up and fished in his pocket for a small velvet box. "Yeah. New year, new season. Time to move things along." He flicked the box open with the cootie finger. A fancy yellow diamond winked fiercely in the firelight. "How about you marry me?"

I took a deep breath. "You do realize we've been together only six months?"

"We can have a long engagement," he said. "Six years, seven. Long as you want."

He slipped the ring easily on my finger. It was the size I usually wore, but it was already a little too large. Soon I would lose so much weight that it would spin like a top. Mitch had heard the oncologist. He saw what I was thinking. Which would come first, the wedding, or the funeral?

"No chemo emo," he said, lifting my chin up. His eyes were smiling. "You will live and not die. Yes or no, will you marry me?"

We kissed until I got dizzy and needed a time-out for club soda. I got up to pour the glasses. When I turned around, I saw that in my brief absence Lars had returned to my fiancé's lap. Mitch was tenderly rototilling the cat's ears.

"Look at him," said Mitch. "Eyes rolled back in his head like he's on the nip."

"He looks like a religious mystic having a fit."

"Saint Lars, Our Kitty of the Perpetual Cootie."

"Heave-ho, Lars," I said, sitting my bald self down in Mitch's lap. "You can get your own miracle. This one's for me."

FIVE

Follow the Wild Goose Flight

How do you tell your PhD friends, far-flung across the world at their various academic postings, that you are attending church *on purpose*? And that it is a conservative church whose views you do not share on several theological points? Can you make your friends understand that for decades you have been thinking at the expense of knowing? That your Inner Skeptic, so busy and reliable all these years, has now earned a time-out? What the Skeptic really deserves is an all-expense-paid vacation to beautiful Costa Rica, but she's gonna have to settle for a noisy Pentecostal church in which passionate teens lip-sync for Jesus while C-walkin' and pop-lockin'.

Don't think I'm kidding. One of the teens, Royce, played God decked out in black pants, festooned with steel chains. With his ripped torso in a skin-tight tee, Royce looked like an advertisement for an S & M magazine. The song was about how we shouldn't bind God to preconceived notions of how God should behave—so we should unchain him, as it were, and let God's mighty freedom refresh our lives! Throughout the song the teens slowly began unchaining Royce/God, who, once unchained, demonstrated his dance brio with commanding creativity there at the altar. The dance had many elements in common with a traditional striptease, but I am hoping that I was the only one who thought so.

Ironic that while I was worried about how to approach my friends with news on the religious front, they were worrying about how to approach me. My friends naturally wished to avoid the tender regrets they would have if I dropped dead before they could wrap things up. They responded to my medical situation with a mournful urgency even though I wasn't mournful. I'm too much like my mother to mind the thought of my own mortality for long. For me the topic of mortality says, "Let's have some rhubarb *Schnetke* and a nice pot of tea."

And anyhow, I've always been good at closure. In college my specialty was writing conclusions. The girls in my dorm all acknowledged that I could conclude any assignment whatsoever, from their lab reports on dendrites to their boring term papers for WOSAM. WOSAM was a real class. It explored the fascinating World of Sage & Messiah. Did I take the class? Hardly! Did I know anything about sages? No! But only a rookie would need to research sages in order to reach a conclusion about them! Sages came from the east, bearing frankincense and myrrh, and that was good enough for me. You may well inquire if cultural underexposure toward the Kings of the Orient exercised any dampening effect on my conclusions. By no means. I handed out conclusions like Halloween candy. I was the MacGyver of conclusions—I could improvise one out of a compass and a piece of string. So don't tell me cancer is all bad!

During chemo I heard from friends I had lost track of and from guys I hadn't dated since 1979. Many friends generously offered to come and take care of me after my mom and sister left. My friend Temperance flew out for a couple of days after a Chicago conference, and she brought her ten-month-old, whom I had never met. Temp and Darin had decided to continue Temp's long family tradition of naming the kids after virtues. They had named the baby Prudence, though I had enthusiastically lobbied for Increase. That was Cotton Mather's father's name in the seventeenth century. I thought it was high time we brought it back.

As a name *Prudence* was altogether too dignified and sedate for this fat-fisted baby. There was nothing prudent about her wholehearted frantic endorsement of tangerine pulp, which she smeared on every available surface. I had to admire this baby's gusto, especially since I was two months into chemo and could no longer contemplate tangerines without projectile vomiting.

Temp was eager to meet Mitch, but she warned us ahead of time that Prudence was strangely standoffish. "She won't go to anybody but me," Temp apologized.

Temp and I were planning to meet Mitch in the parking lot of a cute café. Temp was one of those mothers who don't think twice about propelling their baby into a nice restaurant. Temp remained serene even in the face of airborne cutlery and sudden chuffing raspberries involving watercress-parsnip soup.

Under strict orders not to approach children, I wasn't allowed to hold Prudence. This was hard because she was adorable, with a halo of red-gold hair like her mama. Given

Prudence's reluctance to be held by strangers, I was surprised when in the parking lot Mitch made a slight but commanding gesture to Prudence. He looked enormous and scary; he was wearing dark sunglasses. Yet Prudence instantly responded to his gesture, reaching out eager arms. Mitch took the baby in one big hand, and, with the finesse of long practice, extracted the diaper bag from the backseat with the other. The stroller snapped to attention. Prudence remained placidly on Mitch's lap throughout the lunch. Both Temp and I admired the sureness with which he poked morsels of food from his own plate into Prudence's mouth. She blinked in surprise, but chewed like a trooper.

That night Mitch called to find out how the baby was doing.

"She's sitting on a towel on the hardwood floor. Her head is covered in mashed avocado."

"Right on," he said. "Puttin the moves on an avocado."

Mitch's obvious fondness for babies scored points with my friend. In fact I would say that it sugarcoated the religious pill for Temp, who, like many academics, was an atheist. She had to allow that Mitch was the real thing, a kind man of faith. She observed, moreover, that the kindness and the faith did not exist in his character as independent qualities. Rather, the first was clearly activated by the second. So much was obvious. She was ready to admit that maybe there was something to my idea of giving religion a go. "But if you start persecuting gay people or making predictions about the Second Coming," Temp warned, "I'm going to disown you!"

I told her that Elder Joe had asked Mitch and me to be greeters at church. We had turned down this interesting invitation—I was too sick at the time—but I wanted to see what Temp would say. She frowned and pursed her lips. "A greeter! It's a slippery slope, my friend!"

Then in spring my friends from industry days came out for a visit. Hedda and Thomas are former Los Angeles hipsters who are still riding the wave of Southland political correctness even though they have relocated to Seattle. Seattle, as we know, has its own style of political correctness. Combined with the correctness in LA, where everything you wear or do or order has far-reaching moral implications, the result is not only a guilty conscience, but a desire to share the guilty conscience with one's friends. For example, both Hedda and Thomas, who summer in Italy and who therefore eat dessert, take sugar in their coffee. However, they have assumed a guilty moral position against sugar, due to free-trade issues. This position makes them apologize each and every time they stir a teaspoon of sugar into their coffee. The last time I visited them in Seattle, they had instructed the housekeeper to do the laundry only once a week. She was supposed to dip all the leftover dirty bathwater from the tub into the washing machine. That housekeeper quit, murmuring under her breath, "White folks crazy!" The next two housekeepers also would cut and run when they learned what the job entailed. But finally Hedda secured a housekeeper who was not averse to scooping buckets of grayish bathwater after the children had bathed.

Likewise, Hedda and Thomas had uttered a high-toned, scandalized, "Not on our watch!" when it came to flushing the toilet. When Hedda showed me the bathroom that I would be sharing with her five-year-old, she pointed to a refulgent toilet, lid up, and explained, "If it's yellow, let it mellow. If it's brown, flush it down."

The contents of this toilet were decidedly brown, so I said, "There's a glitch in the system. I think we're overdue for a flush."

She checked me with an outstretched hand. "No, that poop represents Sebastian's decision to save even more water. We're very proud of him. But you can go ahead and flush your own poop, should you desire."

"Thanks," I said.

Meanwhile I was looking forward to seeing more of Sebastian's, um, environmental sensitivity.

The visit was morally uplifting. I was exposed to many edifying new facts about caged poultry, leached vitamins, and sweathouse labor as they related to dinner menus. And that didn't even begin to touch on how Hedda and Thomas felt about church. They didn't like it.

Hedda thought my Mennonite background was quaint. But now that I was a churchgoer, she could not support my religious filiation. Her exact words were, "Honey, has the cancer affected your frontal lobe?" However, Hedda did introduce me to a thrilling new activity. It struck the perfect note between "Congratulations on your engagement!" and "Out, out, brief candle!" Hedda presented me with a set of visualization CDs. A visualization CD is upbeat yet introspective, hopeful yet sober. I was an instant fan. The CDs controverted the passive-patient identity and instead urged listeners to get busy doing something extremely useful, such as falling asleep on the couch.

Hedda's visualization CDs were politically correct from beginning to end. However, someone else gave me one that had a weirdo surprise in the middle, an unexpected turn in the narrative. A woman's voice asked you to get comfy and to start breathing deeply. She'd take you through the usual images: a warm body of water, a sensation of floating, a perfect sunny sky, the fragrance of spicy balsam drifting across the water from the shore. But then the woman's voice said, still in the same hushed matter-of-fact tone, "And now if you direct your attention to the surface of the lake beside you, you will see that a fountain is rising up out of the water. There it is, look!"

My fountain rose.

She continued, "A beautiful spray of healing magical droplets! Gaze at this fountain!"

I gazed.

"Focus on the spray from this fountain. In the stream of crystal droplets you see tiny beings! Their leader tells you it is time to inhale these precious healing droplets deep into your body!"

I always fell asleep after inhaling the tiny magical beings, so who knows how it turned out? But I'd like to think that the tiny beings opened up a new frontier for their kind, there in my renal interior.

It was a resident psychologist at one of my treatment centers who gave me the Tiny Beings CD. To know that this CD bore the stamp of approval from a professional psychologist, one who did not necessarily share my sense of humor, made me like the CD even more. It's very satisfying to sing "Tiny Beings" to the tune of "Tiny Bubbles," in the style of the late Ambassador of Aloha, Don Ho. I recommend this whether or not you have cancer.

Gail the receptionist always asked me to fill out a form that itemized the chemo side effects I was experiencing. My skin turned a curious color, a cross between yellow and green, which, if it were a paint chip, might be called "Peas Porridge Cold." A toxic cloud of chemicals hung in my mouth. Scabrous sores bloomed on my lips.

The drama of the side effects provided a pleasurable contrast with the businesslike tone of the itemized questionnaire. Finger creases popping open like Jimmy Dean Pork Links? Check. Intestinal turbulence, UTIs, cheetah spots? Check, check, check. The best part was a question at the bottom, added like a courteous afterthought. Did I have issues with the cancer? No. Did I need support at home, was I depressed? No, no. Did I need groceries or a babysitter? No, no. On a scale of one to ten, one being the lowest, how did I rate the quality of my life? Once I leaned over to peek at the clipboard of a stage-four patient, a tufted gaunt old lady in down slippers. An oxygen tank sat leashed to her wheelchair like a good dog. Her life was a ten, too. She busted me peeking at her clipboard. We exchanged scrofulous smiles.

I always circled ten unhesitantly, because why claim bad juju? However, I thought I should take advantage of the questionnaire's offer to see the resident psychologist, Dr. Roger. I didn't have a concern per se. Yet why wouldn't I want to pursue every available avenue of healing and well-being?

Hannah thought I wasn't processing my cancer with enough gravity. When she first went with me to meet my chemo oncologist, we had just learned about the size and speed of my tumor. We were ushered into a tiny room, plain as a Pop-Tart.

It offered exactly one low-rent plastic chair, one paper-covered examination bench, and one med cart. The white walls were unadorned except for a single cheap framed Norman Rockwell print called *Before the Shot.* This is the one in which a painfully cute kid in a 1958 doctor's office is bending over, pants lowered. As soon as the nurse left us, I whipped out my little camera and began taking pictures.

"What on earth are you doing?" Hannah asked.

I snapped her exquisitely elegant self sitting in the crappy plastic chair. She was wearing mahogany riding boots and holding an olive Gucci clutch. "Are you kidding? This is no-frills oncology at its finest," I said. "Who's gonna believe the décor in here unless I provide photo documentation?"

My sister cited the No-Frills Oncology as evidence that I needed some cancer-management tips.

When I entered Dr. Roger's dark green lamplit office, the adjutant box of Kleenex at my elbow, I felt as I always did in the offices of psychologists and therapists: worried. Everyone was so suspicious of cheer that I knew I *had* to have a problem. Dr. Roger would probably expect me to cry or express meaningful thoughts on my legacy to family and friends.

On the wall there was a framed print of three wolves running across the tundra in arctic splendor. The wolves seemed to be saying, "It is chilly, we are wolves, let us run!" I wasn't sure how this picture was intended to comment on cancer and hematology. Perhaps it reminded us to cherish our fellow wolves in this the Arctic Winter of our lives. Or maybe it was a paean of praise to the feisty Siberian spirit in seasons of duress. Wolves shall rise, they shall endure, they shall hibernate and have cubs!

After a dignified silence Dr. Roger asked me if there was anything I wanted to tell him. What distressing nadir could I confess? I thought of blurting, "I secretly call my cat Mr. Yummypants!" Instead I thought fast and gave voice to a concern about nutrition. Dr. Roger expressed no surprise at my lackluster problem. He sent me on my way with the Tiny Beings CD and a nice book of cancer recipes. The recipe book I donated to Goodwill, due to a four-month vomitous interlude, but I appreciated the thought.

All around me the oldsters' white blood cells were dropping into the danger zone. I made friends only to miss them. My new chemo buddies would have to take valuable time off their treatment program to recuperate enough for another session in the poison chair. One of the chemo veterans, a frail smoker named Howard, was back in the saddle after a three-month hiatus in which his T cells had languished dangerously low. I loved Howard's bonhomie. He said, chuckling, that cancer was a good disease for him. He'd been bald to begin with.

I was eager to stick to the chemo schedule because I wanted to start renovating Mitch's depressing house. We had decided not to move in together until after the wedding, but this house needed major work. In fact it was this house, rather than the cancer, that would emerge as the more pressing challenge for me. I had seen the hand of blight up close, under Plexiglas. Cancer blackens and shrivels everything in its path. But the cancerous march to the grave is nothing compared to a house you don't like. Mortality is inevitable. We are all required to die as a condition of life. But nobody is required to live in an awful house. Living in an awful house is something we ought to be able to avoid.

This house should not have been awful. It was a spacious home up by the old country club. A solid and respectable structure, it would have been perfect for the bingo couple who favored low ceilings, limited light, and wild-goose wallpaper. The first time I saw the laundry room, the dark epicenter of geese on the wing, I started humming a song we used to sing at Hartland Christian Camp when I was a child:

My paddle's keen and bright,
flashing with silver!
Follow the wild-goose flight,
dip dip and swing!

This song is sung in a round. There is no end. I am here to tell you that once you start singing it, your paddle will be flashing with silver all the livelong day. You will be following the wild-goose flight into the evening hours. I foresaw that doing laundry, a task that I ordinarily like, would become my least favorite chore vis-à-vis these migrating fowl.

Mitch and I agreed that when two midlife adults with separate furnished residences join forces, they should start over, finding a new space and a new rhythm together. Who needs all the karma and complexity of household objects that once belonged to an ex? Trouble is, very few people are in the position to drop their lives and start over. Mitch and I certainly weren't. Thus I would soon be leaving my pretty lake house and confronting, on a daily basis, a sink that made me queasy. Or was that the chemo? You be the judge: this sink was the exact color of plastic violets left on a grave.

Mitch's dad would have been deeply reluctant to move. Albert was totally blind and very hard of hearing, even with two high-tech hearing aids. He had made it clear that he valued the bustling urban center that is Holland, Michigan, a burg of 35,000. But what Albert really loved about Holland was the Maxi Taxi. The Maxi Taxi is a short bus that comes to your door and takes you to the Evergreen Commons Senior Center for a dollar. At eighty-one, Albert conceded to a white cane but refused a guide dog. He didn't want to be seen as disabled. Sometimes he wandered out into the street, cane twitching like a feeler, and we suddenly heard cars screeching to a halt. Although I could have easily hired a student to chauffeur Mitch's dad to and from the Evergreen Commons Senior Center, Albert would have pined for the independence of the Maxi Taxi.

Albert was at his most inspiring in the area of tinfoil. He cherished a complex belief system about mice, whose assumptions I identify as follows:

A. A mouse can fit through a dime-sized crack.
B. The house would be overrun with mice if it were not for many hundreds of tinfoil balls shoved up into the ventilation system.
C. A ball of tinfoil will stop a mouse cold in its tracks.
D. If a hundred balls work okay, thousands work even better.

Can you ever have too many balls of tinfoil shoved up the vent? When I asked Albert if he had ever confirmed a mouse in the house, he shook his head. "No, but you know those mice can squeeze through a crack the size of a dime." He liked the idea of the dime-sized crack. He was sticking with it.

A milk-tea seventies brick exterior had yellowed to the color of old underpants. Two shrinkydink windows suggested slits in a citadel. The overall effect from the curb was one of dark paranoia, as when a family of couch potatoes makes a pact never to leave the large-screen TV in the basement. Mitch's house was flanked on either side by two homes with cheerful curb appeal—cozy Adirondacks arranged tête à tête, colorful Japanese maples, well-tended flower beds. And Mitch's place was also neat as a pin. Yet it looked like what it was: the house of a man with a fake leather couch. And on that couch, an acrylic throw. And on that throw, a realistic deer head. This deer head was twice as large as it should have been, and much more festive, as if it had only recently stopped nodding to the tune of "Here We Go Looby-Loo." When I first saw the deer-head throw, my heart sank. This was worse than the massive flagpole in the middle of the lawn.

And that wasn't even considering the horse.

In the corner to the immediate left of the garage stood a white ceramic horse about four feet tall. It had a quizzical, not to say inimitable, expression hand-painted on its face. Its eyebrows said, "Good people, gather ye plenty of canned goods for the Apocalypse!" This horse had a mysterious little smile like the Mona Lisa, and its eyes followed you as you got out of your car. The horse rose up boldly on hind legs. Its rearing presence in front of the garage defied all reason, but it was the first thing you saw from the driveway.

I was so appalled when I first saw it that for months I could say nothing whatsoever. Who would put that horse in front of their *personal home*, and under what circumstances? Did it have something to do with Mitch's years as a drug dealer? Had his ex-wife selected it the way some people display gnomes with droopy pants, as if gnome fannycrack is something we all want to see? I agonized about how to bring this horse up in casual conversation.

My mother beat me to it. The first time we drove her to Mitch's house, as we were pulling into the driveway, Mom leaned up from the backseat to administer an astonished poke to my upper arm. I turned. Her eyebrows shot up, like the flagpole. At no point did she pause to struggle with tact. "Mitch," she said, "what on earth is the story with that horse?" She stretched a finger horseward, pointing.

"You like it?" he asked.

"No," she said decisively. "I'm pretty sure no woman alive likes it."

"It was here when we moved in. That thing's too heavy to move. Two- or three-man job for sure."

I threw my mother a grateful look. To Mitch I said, "I know people! I'll bribe some strapping college students to come in the dead of night and make it go away." Cosmic forces might persuade me to live in a house I didn't pick, but embrace this creepy horse I would never do.

Mitch's house overlooked a beautiful ravine in the back. Yet how could a woodsy ravine make up for the fact that I would have to live in a gloomy basement whose ceiling was eight inches above my head? Albert, who was blind, lived upstairs, where there was more light. Mitch and Leroy occupied the darker downstairs, which featured plastic wood paneling and gym equipment in the living room. I do not know what logic dictated this arrangement. But one thing was clear. Four of the basement rooms, including the kitchen, did not have a single window.

Albert saw no need for change, particularly if a thing had been functional for at least thirty years. For instance, many years earlier Albert's wife, Delores, had paid to have a dark film installed on the windows. Albert believed that this dark film saved money on the heating bill. When Mitch told me that the house was dark on purpose, I helplessly made the sign of the cross. Maybe these *are* the end times. Doesn't the book of Revelation mention people who put dark films in their windows? And even if it doesn't, the reverse certainly holds. People who put dark films in their windows certainly mention the book of Revelation.

Delores passed away in 2003 at age seventy-five, though Mitch tells me she seemed seventy-five even when he was a little boy. All through his marijuana years she had been a stern hovering presence in polyester leisure suits, quick on the draw with chunky Jell-O desserts and canned asparagus. But Delores had been gone for years, and Albert theoretically wanted to move on. He was dating, and there was nothing we loved more than seeing him suited up in his turquoise 1960s sportcoat, hair crisped with Vitalis. "Do my socks match?" he'd ask. "I'm taking LaVerna out for pot roast at the hospital cafeteria!"

Albert said he wanted a new wife, but he was unwilling to let go of the old one. One of the most basic foundational truths of moving on after the breakup or death of a loved one is: get rid of the stuff. Do a clean sweep. Start over. The idea is that material reminders of the ex, such as furniture, pictures, and curios, keep you psychologically committed to that ex. It's hard to reach out a hand to receive new opportunities when with the other hand you're clutching onto the past. Albert had dated several nice senior ladies, but the presence of Delores was still all over his personal space. Delores had covered every available surface in the house with old-lady gimcracks, and it looked as if Albert had retained them all, from ceramic pumpkins to ancient soaps in the shape of a gardenia to Kleenex holders crocheted to resemble an antebellum hoopskirt.

Mitch hadn't really noticed all the plastic seashells, the squirrel nutkins, the merbabies made of cornhusks. It wasn't that Mitch had bad taste. It was that he had no taste. Furniture just happened to him. When his parents became too frail to care for each other, Mitch drove down to Florida, boxed up all the Jell-O molds and coupon holders, and moved his folks into the big house. He installed handicap rails in the bathrooms and never looked back.

Mitch lived his life as if his home were completely tangential to the events that transpired there. It had been so long since I had been with a straight guy that I was amazed by all the things Mitch didn't see. This was a man who might miss a ¾″ full-bodied spider on the ceiling. When I called his attention to it, he reached up and killed it with his thumb. "Djhgge!" he said, making the noise of metal crunching, as from *Terminator*.

Although Mitch had no clear idea how depressing his house was, he could see that the move was going to be hard for me. He therefore gave me what turned out to be another perfect gift: a pledge to be as flexible as possible. Like the Yamaha keyboard,

Mitch's gift would assume value as I lived with it. It would grow so dear, and make me feel so cherished, that soon I would be marveling at the gift this ugly house had made possible.

I won't say it was easy to renovate a house I didn't like. And I won't say that I accepted the result as a long-term residence. But Mitch's attitude encouraged me to look at what I would have (a man of amazing generosity), as opposed to what I wouldn't have (an attractive, sunny house). Mitch promised that he would help me bring beauty to his home as long as we could make the changes on our shoestring budget, and as long as we paid cash for every single project. So as my chemo schedule allowed, we plunged into a cloud of primer, drywall, and peeling wallpaper. Seafoam bedroom, begone! Fake fireplace log, hasta la vista! Unspeakable laminate, Djhgge!

"Do you like this color for the master bedroom?" I asked, waving a paint swatch. "It's called 'Rich Cashmere.'"

"Yeah."

"Which do you like more, Rich Cashmere or Stifled Sigh?"

"I like whichever you like."

It took a while for the depth and breadth of his gift to sink in. Then it seemed all the sweeter that he was putting every spare moment into a project he cared nothing about. He was doing all this for *me*. Soberly, steadily, walls were painted. Showers were regrouted. Floors were tiled. It turned out that Mitch could do everything, from hardwiring light fixtures to changing toilets to installing gas lines. Whenever I suggested calling in a pro to save time, he'd frown and say, "Nah, we don't need no pro. Fixin things comes easy to me. I feel the same way about plumbers as you do about store-bought pie."

We bought a big streamlined sink for the master bath. I said, "It's such a great sink. Too bad we have to put it on a counter that comes up to my thigh."

He looked at the counter and scratched his head. "I can build that up. No sense in havin a counter too low for the both of us." And true to his word, he raised the surface by a cool half foot and fitted out the front of the cabinet with a sleek powder-coated stainless-steel panel. Things were looking up. We were slowly creating for ourselves a comfy little nest, clean and modern.

During these months I was thinking, "How hard can caring for an elderly parent be?" Friends in similar circumstances shared delightful stories. My friend Carla's dad, who was ninety, had Alzheimer's. There was a tenderness that crept into Carla's voice when she talked about her dad. This old gent had lived exclusively in Tennessee and Alabama all his life, and he had never traveled. But as the Alzheimer's advanced, he grew increasingly oracular on the subject of domestic travel. I found Carla's dad's geographic ideation wonderfully refreshing. For example, after a fellow Alzheimer's patient named Henrietta had pushed him, he declared, "From now on I'm gonna stay on the Arkansas side of the house!" Carla and I weren't sure what this meant, but we liked it.

Once Carla arrived at the care facility when the staff was in a panicky brouhaha. Her father had mysteriously vanished. Carla joined the search. She finally found her dad crouched beneath one of the tables in the dining room. She moved the tablecloth and bent to help him get up. "What are you doing down there, Dad?" she asked.

"Resting. Have they stopped all that shooting?"

"No one's shooting. Are you ready for your haircut now?"

He nodded tractably. "Sure hope it don't hurt like that time in California."

Sometimes Carla bites, sometimes she doesn't. This one made her take a deep breath. "One, Dad, it's *hair*. It doesn't hurt. Two, you've never been to California."

"I have so."

"No you haven't."

"Have so."

"California, known for splendors such as the Hollywood Walk of Fame, the Golden Gate Bridge, and haircuts!"

"I got a haircut once in California," he persisted.

"When?"

"That time I went out there to get my hair cut."

"Oh my God. At this minute I am arguing with my ninety-year-old dad about whether he had his hair cut in California. This is my life."

"Better than the life I had in upstate New York."

Carla's tone always said, "What's not to love about a dad who thinks he has traveled to thirty-six of the continental United States?" I did get it that taking care of her dad was hard. Imagine lying helplessly in your bed in Michigan while a strangely young and vigorous Alzheimer's patient named Henrietta is knocking your frail old dad to the floor, fracturing his pelvis. You'd feel as helpless as the old guy.

In spite of the difficulty, and the helplessness of seeing a beloved parent age, it seemed to me that the caregiving relationship would also offer many opportunities to give and receive joy. Living with Albert, I thought, would be a delicious experience. I didn't imagine anything would make it difficult to cherish the man who had adopted my husband.

Like Carla's dad, my own parents were adventurous and merry of heart. Since my father's retirement nine years earlier he had entropically fused to his raspberry leather easy chair, yet he was still willing to follow my mother into the wilds of Alaska, Panama, the Sudan, you name it. What is it that fills old people with wanderlust? My folks toured the Middle East with fearless indifference to the National Terrorism Advisory System. Everywhere my mother went she was followed at the heel by a frisky little carry-on, like a puppy. Onto the black fabric she had affixed a large letter J—J for Janzen—with electrical tape. Mom and Dad shared this carry-on, often as their only suitcase, and away they went. They liked fellowshipping with international Mennonites, and they were all about sampling thousand-year-old eggs and yak butter tea.

"Yak butter tea!" I said. "What did it taste like?"

"Like slippery urine," Mom said, shuddering. "In Tibet we drank it at every meal."

"If it was so bad, why'd you keep drinking it?"

"Well, when in Rome. What would life be if you didn't try new things?"

My parents had spent a lifetime making people feel good about urinous tea. More to the point, they had resolutely taken responsibility for their own happiness. My father was wise in counsel, long on Bermuda shorts. My mother always had a kind word on her lips or a sausage in her purse. If in the middle of a day of errands you expressed hunger, she'd rummage and produce a partially smooshed baggie, perhaps with a cough drop stuck to it. "Here's half a nice cabbage bun! It's a little hot from the car, but perfectly edible!" It wasn't that they were always giving you half a cabbage bun with a cough drop. It was that they really, truly, from the bottom of their hearts, wanted you to have it. If you ask me, my parents set the bar pretty high.

Unlike my parents, Albert did not appear to be enjoying himself. He was a good-looking old bird, with a full head of snow-white hair and a movie star's craggy chin. In fact he looked like Michael Douglas, except that, being blind, he favored a ladies' pink-and-white-striped knit winter hat. It had a confetti pom-pom on top. The only thing that could have improved this hat was a Hello Kitty patch. There were many things I admired about Albert, and his willingness to wear this hat was one of them. Mitch had told him over and over that no self-respecting man would wear a ladies' pink-striped pom-pom hat, but Albert had a neat system. If he didn't see it, he didn't mind it. It reminded me of women with VPL, visible panty lines, whom I also admired as forward thinkers. No looking back!

Albert lived with resourceful thrift on his investment income and Social Security. Every week he insisted on buying his own groceries. I loved it that, although he was computer literate, he always handwrote his grocery list, confident in his blindness that he was expressing himself with succinct legibility. The perusal of this list was an utter crapshoot. A crazy downhill squiggle might translate as "Banquet frozen dinner." The mysterious "herb tisane" was actually "hair dressing." What I felt might be "candy chocolate donut" turned out to be "ladies' swimming bonnet."

Albert demonstrated his independence with a commitment to on-sale TV dinners, frozen breakfast sandwiches, and potted luncheon meat. He could have had homemade meals whenever I made dinner at Mitch's, but eating at his son's table would have made him feel too dependent. A blind and deaf man needs to exert his independence. At the same time I couldn't stand the thought of him never getting any good kitchen lovin'.

So I pressed him to join us for the occasional meal. Whenever he did, he followed the same pattern. At first he'd decline any unfamiliar food. If I identified roasted sweet-potato fries on his plate at four o'clock, he'd answer that he didn't care for sweet potatoes, thank you. By then I had learned to ask, "Did Delores use to fix yams with marshmallow cream and brown sugar?" When Albert would nod, delicately grimacing, I'd urge him, momlike, to try just one bite. And although he never admitted that he liked the new food, he'd take seconds and Saran-wrap what he couldn't finish. "Course I like to eat at 5:30 evenings," he'd say, when I told him we were eating at 6:00.

I winced when Albert's list requested waxy Little Debbie cakes, prefab cherry turnovers, and cookies rubbery with preservatives. As often as I could, I'd bring him homemade treats.

"Albert, here are a couple of fresh caramel cookies at two o'clock," I'd say, setting the plate down beside him. "I made them this morning."

"I don't want any cookies right now. At the fair they were giving away free cookies to all the seniors."

"Should I take them away?"

"No, no, leave them there. I'll eat them later."

He ate my offerings, but grudgingly, always on his terms. Or—what do I know?—maybe he waited until I was gone and scraped my food into the garbage disposal. When I'd return, I'd find the empty saucer, washed and dried, on the bar of the downstairs kitchen. It was hard not to read the round O of the saucer as a zero, a comment on the nullity of the connection I had tried to make. What was I doing wrong? I had tried to do him a favor, but the plate seemed to suggest a reversal, that Albert was the one doing me the favor, eating food he hadn't requested and didn't want.

And so I'd put the plate away in the windowless kitchen, telling myself that the development of rapport was a process, a matter of time and patience. I would take as my model the indefatigable geese from the hideous wallpaper in the laundry room. Like them, I'd move according to season. Wild yet domestic, free yet contained, these geese flew in endless peregrinations around the laundry room. I could do that. Dip, dip, and swing.

SIX

The Ghost in the Tub

When Mitch was five years old, just in time to appreciate really big cockroaches, Albert and Delores moved to Naples, Florida. Mitch's first memory of Poinciana Village was the palmetto bugs, so large they'd sometimes scrabble at the door, too big to slide under. When the family pulled up to the new tract home, a big palmetto bug lay clicking and buzzing on its back on the front porch. This palmetto bug Mitch interpreted as a personal gift and a good omen. He remembers it as being half the size of his foot, and he stomped it crunchily, pleased at the way things were shaping up in Florida.

Albert had driven a U-Haul packed with the family's worldly goods, and they had stopped at a building site in Naples to hire some men standing around in the street to come and help unload. As soon as Albert had unlocked the front door, Delores went from room to room, closing the blinds against the bright afternoon. Albert turned on an overhead fan that began to stir the humid air.

Just as the unemployed men were wrestling Delores's big

Technics organ from the U-Haul, a towheaded boy flashed by on a bike, pedaling furiously, hands in the air. Mitch and this boy made eye contact, and the boy looped back around on the sidewalk. Enter Billy Pilcher, who was at that very moment debuting his new Schwinn Orange Crate. Billy was six, old enough for a slick wide tire, banana seat, and three-speed shift on the bar.

Billy paused on the sidewalk to watch the unemployed men unload the stiff floral hide-a-bed sofa. Mitch ran down the porch steps. Billy waved him over. "I got this here Schwinn Orange Crate," he said. "Lookit the three-speed shift."

"Whoa."

"You got a bike?"

Mitch nodded unhappily. His bike was not a Schwinn Orange Crate, but a no-speed crappy small-seater that his dad had bought at a garage sale. It had hard tires and a stiff plastic seat in an embarrassing color: burgundy.

Billy Pilcher spat thoughtfully on the sidewalk. "My tooth is loose, lookit."

Mitch inspected the loose tooth.

"We could ride our bikes out to the irrigation ditches. Sometimes gars go swimming through 'em in packs."

"What's a gar?"

"A fish, dummy. You a 'tard or what?"

"No, I'm from Michigan."

The boys sized each other up. They were satisfied. This exchange would become the foundation of a friendship that would make up in intimacy what it lacked in length. Soon Billy and Mitch would be raining down a holy hell of pebbles on the gars, or riding alongside the truck that came to spray for mosquitoes. It kicked out a dense white pesticide that Mitch and Billy cheerfully ingested as they grabbed the bumper. One damp July afternoon Mitch rose considerably in Billy's estimation. Mitch managed to convince Billy's little sister Jayleen that a headless and legless palmetto bug was a piece of Russell Stover candy. These boys liked each other fine, yes sir.

Albert had moved his family to Florida for his wife's health. Her doctor in Michigan had said she needed a warm climate. Once a nurse, Delores had long stopped working due to severe arthritis and back problems. At thirty-nine she was fully inhabiting the invalid role she would push like a walker throughout her life. When I asked Albert if Delores had already needed her walker at Poinciana Village, he said, "No, not at that time. But she was taking a lot of pain pills." Delores did have real pain, and a real illness. But she was also one of those sufferers who cranked it up a notch.

There's a ten-dollar word for a person who fixates on aches and pains: *valetudinarian.* I'm not saying that valetudinarians are hypochondriacs, because plenty of them, like Delores, have actual illnesses. The thing that distinguishes the valetudinarian is that the illness, real or imagined, prevents the sufferer from living life to the fullest. The valetudinarian is really saying, "Polly wants a cracker! Give me love for my migraine and/or sleep disorder!"

It was a literal case of the blind leading the lame. Six months after the move to Poinciana Village, Delores would be alternating between walker and wheelchair, and Albert would be legally blind. Born in 1930 and 1931, both Albert and Delores embraced what must have been familiar gender roles to them—he the caretaker, she the martyr.

Once I asked Albert if he loved Delores. He smiled drily and said, "Marriage means you do what you need to do." Albert had met her through an early Christian singles organization. Before he began a written correspondence with Delores, two other women had broken up with him. One of those women had even ended an engagement with him. When this woman found out that Albert's degenerative blindness was hereditary, she decided to take a pass, for the sake of the future children. Delores was less choosy. Delores had already had a hysterectomy, and she was fine with the idea of adopting. When I asked Albert what attracted him to Delores, he said with a simplicity that made me want to reach out and kiss him, "Delores was just willing to go out with me, is all. I drove all the way up to Saginaw, Michigan, from where I lived in Chillicothe, Ohio. That was a five-hour drive."

Mitch never offered much information about his mom. I naturally pointed this out because I am always talking about my own mother. Recognizing the truth of this, he paused to search for memories. He then got that careful look that meant he wanted to watch what kind of words were coming out of his mouth. "My mama's personality was sort of hard to see. She took a lot of pain meds."

"Would I have liked her? Would she have liked me?"

"She wasn't like your mama, honey. No joy in her spirit."

"Oh."

Albert's visual impairment had begun when he was a teenager. One night he went coon hunting with his cousins, and he wondered at their speed and confidence in navigating through the dense woods—the cousins, not the coons. Though apparently the raccoons were also more sure-sighted than he. In his twenties he was already wearing glasses with a built-in hearing aid. His doctor told him that he was suffering from the degenerative disease we now call retinitis pigmentosa, with Usher's syndrome. The impairment he was already experiencing, said the doctor, would give way to total blindness by the time he was sixty. Mysteriously, neither Albert's parents nor any of his grandparents had had vision problems. A girl cousin had been diagnosed with multiple sclerosis, and her eyesight was weak, but otherwise he was alone in his disability. Twenty years before the doctor predicted, Albert was declared legally blind. He was just forty years old, six months into the new house in Poinciana Village.

"How did you see to drive the U-Haul?" I asked.

"Retinitis pigmentosa narrows your vision, like in a tunnel. I couldn't see around the sides, but I could still see straight to drive."

On one of the rare occasions when Delores felt well enough to take an evening walk in the neighborhood, Albert and Delores met Billy Pilcher's parents. Mrs. Pilcher had blond hair, stacked in an attractive bouffant. She was sitting on the porch, combing leave-in cream rinse into Jayleen's pale hair.

"Ouch, Mama, you're hurting me."

"Hold still, sweetie."

"That's Mitch's mom and dad," Jayleen said, pointing at their slow progress on the sidewalk. "His mama walks funny."

"Shh, that's not polite." Mrs. Pilcher rose, wiped her cream-rinse hand on her slacks, and went down the walk to meet Albert and Delores.

"I suppose it's high time we met," Mrs. Pilcher said cheerfully. "Since the boys spend every lovin' minute of every day together! I'm Trisha Pilcher."

"Albert, call me Al. My wife, Delores."

"I know my husband'll want to meet you. Hang on." Trisha Pilcher ran lightly back to the screen door and called in, "Hon, come meet Mitch's parents!"

There were more handshakes all around. It turned out that the Pilchers were Methodists, perfectly pleasant, but Methodists. Albert and Delores were Baptists. They exchanged small talk, wished each other well, and returned to their separate evening orbits.

On a Tuesday in July Albert clocked out of his job as case-worker for the Florida Division of Family Services. He had worked a full day and stayed on the job until exactly five o'clock, as he always did. (I don't know about the God of the Methodists, but the God of the Baptists appreciated crisp time management.) Albert got into his big white '59 Ford Galaxy 500 and began to drive home from the division office in Naples. A light sprinkle had just commenced when Albert turned onto the T that dead-ended into Poinciana Village. Ahead on the sidewalk he saw Billy Pilcher on his Schwinn, riding full tilt, talking back over his shoulder to another little boy on a bike. Suddenly Billy swooped out into the road, still looking backward over his shoulder.

Albert slammed on the brakes, willing himself not to hear the soft thud. Billy went flying twenty-six feet from the point of impact. He landed on his head on the left curb. Albert cut the engine and ran toward him, shouting, "Are you okay? Billy, Billy, are you okay?"

Billy was conscious. He raised his head and blinked. "I guess," he said.

The little boy on the other bike was Mitch, who saw his father hit his friend so hard that the little body rose high into the air. Mitch doesn't remember the ambulance that came to take Billy away to the hospital in Naples. All he remembers is Billy's mom, screaming from the front porch, running down the lawn, crouching on her heels beside her son in the rain. She was sobbing and hysterically repeating, "BillyBillyBillyBillyBilly." The Orange Crate Schwinn lay twisted in the street.

That night Albert slept restlessly. Delores, self-medicating, had taken an extra pain pill to sleep through the panic. Billy Pilcher might die, and if he did, her own husband would have killed him. Delores was therefore sleeping the deep sleep of prescription narcotics.

At 1:15 a.m. Albert lay blinking at the ceiling, wide awake, heart pounding. Something had awakened him, but he wasn't sure what. He snapped on the bedside light, then the overhead. Beside him Delores sighed and rolled like a wave breaking on a shallow beach. Nothing seemed untoward or out of place. But his heart was still pounding, crazily now, as if something were about to happen. He snapped back the covers and thought, "This is ridiculous." He would get up and use the restroom. On his way down the hall he stopped and cracked open the door of Mitch's room. Mitch lay curled up like a Cheeto, having fallen asleep with his little fist around the Hot Wheels Billy had given him for his birthday.

As Albert approached the bathroom, the hair on his arms lifted. He was not a man for hunches, or mysterious chills, or inner knowings, but he knew that something wasn't right. Something in the bathroom was wrong, all wrong.

The door was cracked. He pushed it. No resistance—except that the prickles multiplied along his arms. He quickly turned on the light. And rubbed his eyes. All around him the bathroom was filled with a dense white mist that hung like a tule fog, opaque and motionless. Albert waved his arms through it. It didn't feel wet, just thick. The fog utterly whited out the mirror over the sink. Zero visibility. Albert reached out to touch the glass, to see if the fog was a kind of steam or condensation. It wasn't. Then he felt for the shower door. He couldn't see his own hand inches in front of his face, but the shower walls were dry inside and out. This was the first time he stood in utter blindness, the white fog a sign of what was to come.

Blinking and confused, he slowly became aware that here in this bathroom, on a hot August night, he was cold. Really cold. In fact it was like a freezer in there. And this wasn't a good cold, a refreshing cold on a hot and humid night. It was a dry, illogical, inexplicable, bone-chilling cold.

He beat a hasty retreat, pulling the door solidly shut behind him. Had the mist filled other rooms? He turned on the hall light, but the hall was clear and hot, just like the rest of the house. From under the bathroom door came a tendril of the cold white mist, as if sending out an exploratory feeler. Teeth chattering, he walked with alacrity down the hall and back to bed, piling on the blankets that Dolores in her sleep had rejected.

What was hovering in the bathroom? This would become the

only experience of his life that he could not account for. Albert was a rational man. He had a college education and a firm, businesslike mind. For pleasure he read books on finance, or nice cowboy Westerns.

The next morning the police detective came by before breakfast to tell them that Billy had died in the night.

"What time?"

"They called it at 1:15. The Pilchers are distraught, as you can imagine. But they're worried about you. They've asked their minister to stop by later today and see how you're doing. They want you to know they understand what happened. And anyway we've already measured the braking distance. There was no way you could have stopped in time."

"No."

"You wouldn't have had time to stop at a bar between when you left work and the time of the accident." He checked his pad. "McFarland says you clocked out at exactly 5:01." This logic seemed airtight to the police detective. And anyway, Albert said that he was a churchgoing Baptist man; he didn't drink.

With Delores hovering anxiously in the background, the police detective took Albert's statement and asked him many follow-up questions. As he was leaving, he handed Albert a packet of optional papers to fill out. "Guess you'll be feeling pretty bad," said the detective. "I want to stress that you are under no obligation to fill these out. It's not mandatory. Your statement is enough. Been there myself. Once while I was driving in downtown Miami, a little boy, just a wee shaver, darted out from between two parked cars and I hit him. He just ran out without looking, poor mite."

"Was he killed?" Delores leaned in to ask.

The detective nodded. "Bad times."

Neither the state police detective nor the insurance representative asked Albert about his vision impairment. Why should they? He was legally licensed to drive.

The minister came by as promised, faithfully conveying that the Pilchers were not seeking to blame Albert for Billy's death. They knew their son had been riding fast without looking, and over and over Trisha had warned him not to swoop kamikaze-like into the street. The minister did not offer to pray with Albert and Delores. They said to themselves: "He is Methodist."

Albert, who had been narrating all this to me forty-one years after the fact, fell silent. He tipped his handsome head back in his chair, hands on the armrests.

"That's the end of the story?" I asked loudly.

"Yes."

"Did you go to the funeral? What happened with the insurance? How did Mitch handle Billy's death?"

"Mitch was young. He got over it. We thought it would be inappropriate to go to the funeral, especially since Billy's older sister blamed me. Nothing happened with my insurance except that my insurance company sent the Pilchers some money toward the funeral arrangements. A couple thousand dollars. I asked why they did that, because it made it look like an admission that I was at fault."

"What'd they say?"

"They said the check was just a gesture of support to bereaved parents."

"What happened with the car?"

"The car?"

"Did the insurance pay to fix it?"

"My car was fine. Nothing wrong with it."

That made me tear up for a moment. That an indifferent instrument of death should be fine while a little boy had been killed! But I went back, as Albert must have known I would, to the fog in the bathroom.

"Did you think the fog in the bathroom was Billy's ghost?"

"I wouldn't say that," said Albert. "Can't say as I knew what it was. Just that it was spooky."

"I wonder why Billy's ghost would have appeared in the bathroom, as opposed to some other room," I said.

Leroy strolled in, texting furiously. With one eye on his phone he said over his shoulder that in the movies ghosts always appeared in the bathroom. "That's what ghosts *do*. You look in the mirror and there they are, standing right behind you."

I thought of my own childhood fear of haunted bathrooms and nodded. "Maybe the bathroom invites fears of supernatural visitation because it's a place of extreme vulnerability. We're looking at our most naked selves, doing our most private activities, and so the bathroom becomes a symbol of self-examination. Every bathroom has a mirror. We look in those without our makeup or clothes to see our truest selves. And what are ghosts but the projection of our own complex anxieties?"

Leroy laughed politely. "I seen this movie where Michelle Pfeiffer sees this girl's ghost in the bathtub. She was trying to tell Michelle Pfeiffer where her body was. Harrison Ford drowned her in the lake. It was so cool."

"Why didn't the girl ghost just tell Michelle Pfeiffer straight out? Why did she have to appear in the bathtub?"

"Because a bathtub is filled with water. Like a lake," Leroy explained. "That's why the ghost appeared in the bathtub. Because she drowned in the *lake*."

"Got it," I said.

"Okay, see ya, Jag's picking me up for band practice."

"Who drowned in the lake?" asked Albert.

"Nobody," I said. "Leroy was talking about a ghost."

"Leroy, did you see a ghost?"

"He's gone to band practice, Albert," I said loudly.

"Course ghosts have never been documented," he said.

"If the white mist wasn't Billy's ghost, what was it?"

"Can't say. Spooky, though."

All that afternoon, painting trim in the sunroom, I thought about Albert's sad story. When Mitch came home from work, I promptly shucked my paint hoodie so that I could plaster myself against him. "Today your daddy told me the story about killing Billy Pilcher," I said, nuzzling Mitch's neck. He spread his hand on my pate and kissed me with elaborate care in one of the safety zones. He was getting good at alternative caresses.

"Was it sad like you thought? You were pretty worked up about it the first time I told you."

"He narrated it just as you would tell any old story," I said. "I don't think he finds it as poignant as I do."

"Lotta disappointment and defeat in his life. Goin blind.

Goin deaf. Adoptin a kid and then havin him turn out to be an alcoholic drug dealer."

"Being married to a woman he didn't love. Tending her for thirty years when he himself needed care. Killing Billy Pilcher."

Mitch rubbed his scratchy chin on my cheek. "Billy was hot-doggin on that bike. Seems to me that Billy was the one responsible for killin Billy."

"Still. The guilt. Think of carrying that around with you for forty years."

"Goes a long way to explain why my daddy's so negative all the time."

People always ask where God is in the midst of suffering. To me it's a strange question. When you go blind, when a neighbor kills your son, when you come down with a spanking case of cancer, God is in exactly the same place where he always is. He's where you put him. The thing about *liberum arbitrium*, free will, is that God respects our right to choose. Do we want to connect with him, or do we want to live a life without him? We get to pick. If in the midst of our suffering, we call on God to sustain us, then that's where God will be. If, on the other hand, we choose to weather life's storms without seeking God's presence, we can do that. I opted for the latter strategy for twenty-some years.

I suppose when people ask where God is in suffering, what they really mean is, "Why doesn't God *prevent* human suffering?" The specious underlying assumption is, "If God existed at all, he would prevent human suffering." I have never understood this position. None of the world religions promises fewer problems for people of faith. In fact every major world religion observes that suffering is inevitable and constitutive. We suffer as part of the human condition. Think about it: if we didn't suffer, would we still be human? Consider how much consciousness would change. If we didn't suffer, we would be unable to choose a response to suffering, and so would forfeit sentience.

Choosing how to respond to life is our greatest responsibility, and our greatest freedom. And although it was none of my business, I was saddened by how Albert had chosen. For most of the day Albert sat passive in his chair. Books on tape made him sleepy. When he wasn't napping, he checked the weather, he locked the doors, he closed the curtains. Twice a week he went to Evergreen Commons Senior Center for water aerobics. Come hell or high water, he vacuumed every Monday and Friday morning. But his boredom was a palpable thing. It lay like a stretch of wet cement that he protected with cones and tape. Every time we made suggestions—Take a class! Learn a language! Study piano! Try sudoku!—he found objections aplenty. And his negativity went further than merely shooting down our suggestions. Like Eeyore, he always found a way to undermine a good report. His rejoinders weren't mean-spirited. They were just quietly, persistently negative.

If I said, "Good news, the Realtor's showing my house today at 2:00," he would say, "Course nobody's buying in this economy." If Mitch left the front door unlocked for a moment, Albert would say, "While ago a car was stolen right out of a garage, not three blocks away." When I'd ask Albert how things were going with his girlfriend, he'd say, "LaVerna doesn't want to get married. She told me to stop talking about it."

I told him that under those circumstances I would speak life and health into that relationship by privately declaring every single day that LaVerna *did* want to get married, and that she was now setting the date.

Albert's dry half-smile told me that he found this counsel as silly as it was amusing. Speaking positive outcome over a situation that smelled bleak represented a failure to live in the real world. Albert was proud of his ability to face facts. By jingo, he would never dwell in the hazy romantic glow of mere possibility! Although still a practicing Baptist, Albert didn't believe in miracles, or healing, or the laying on of hands. He told me once that his blindness was a cross God wanted him to bear with long-suffering and acceptance. True enough: Albert's words both predicted and delivered exactly what he was experiencing. Sometimes when I saw Albert sitting motionless in his chair, I thought, paraphrasing Saint Paul in Philippians, "For I have learned the secret of resignation in all things..." Albert sought neither joy nor contentment. Consequently he experienced neither. At day's end, when Mitch crossed the threshold with thermos and lunchbox, Albert would throw down a fistful of complaints that he had been hanging on to all day, as when you are sometimes forced to walk a distance before you find a trash can for your sticky wrappers.

I tried to tell myself that the spirit of kvetch was understandable, given the onus of Albert's disability. But in my heart I knew that nobody has to be a crankypants. Kvetching is a choice. You can choose to do it, or you can choose not to. Once when Mitch, frustrated, pointed out Albert's chronic negativity, Albert astonishingly tried to make a biblical case for it. He cited the eleventh chapter of the Gospel of Luke. This story is called the Parable of the Friend at Midnight. A man knocks on his friend's door in the middle of the night, asking for three loaves of bread. The sleepy friend shouts from inside the house, "It's late, go away!" Jesus suggests that if the sleeper is a true friend, he'll eventually get out of bed and pony up the three loaves. The point of the parable is that God, a true friend, will provide for us when we ask him to. Personally, I would not have read this story as an injunction to be unpleasant to my family members, but so it goes. Albert concluded, "So there's biblical precedent for nagging!" He meant it, too.

Most in-home caregivers deal with more challenging problems than a spirit of kvetch. For instance, it would have been much harder to watch a beloved parent slip into dementia, or to humiliate a venerable elder with brisk diaper changes. If that had been our situation, an assisted-living facility might have been the answer. But Albert wanted to stay right where he was. Besides, there was nothing physically wrong with him aside from his vision and hearing impairment. Mitch and I wanted to cherish him; he was our elder, a father figure, and as such we wanted to provide a home in which he could be comfortable. However, as I saw more of the dynamic between him and Mitch in the months before the wedding, I had to bite my tongue. Thank God for Mr. Wurby's sand displacement! I intoned out loud, over and over, "I am happy and grateful that Albert is mentally sharp and physically spry."

How should you pray for a dad who does not appear to respect or even like his own son? How do you pray for an eighty-one-year-old man who can always be counted on to say the one negative thing there is to be said?

In his gorgeous book *Celebration of Discipline*, Richard Foster says that if we are to progress in our spiritual walk, we must "lay down the everlasting burden of always needing to manage others." If anybody was going to change, it would have to be me. I said as much to Mitch, who nodded. "My daddy's the sole person in charge of what comes out of his mouth," he said. "Nothin we can do about any of that. All we can ever do is clean up our own side of the street. Plus it don't matter that he don't love me overmuch. It's my assignment to respect him."

Not much you can do when your parent finds you more useful than interesting. Mitch went off to respect his father by giving him a haircut, high and tight, with an electric clipper fully fifty years old. Albert requested this haircut every three or four weeks whether he needed it or not. He liked to set everything up in the middle of the kitchen the day before. Because he checked the length of his hair at thirty-second intervals, the ancient wheeze of the clipper came and went like the west wind. I stepped over the waiting bullet-shaped "vacuum machine," as Albert called it. Its aqua plastic shell must have been all the crack in 1961.

Albert was twiddling two super-short tufts of white hair at either temple. He had removed his hearing aids and couldn't hear us.

"Oh honey," I said. "That's too short on the sides. He looks like Hitler."

Mitch grinned and gestured open-palmed toward his father, not unlike a game-show host introducing a brand-new La-Z-Boy. Without the hearing aids Albert couldn't gauge his volume. He shouted, like a war cry, "Shorter on the sides!"

In response to me Mitch adapted the serenity prayer of Saint Francis. "God grant me the serenity to accept the Hitler haircuts I cannot change, and the wisdom to know what I *can* change. And the courage to know the difference."

"Hey," I said over my shoulder from the laundry room, where I was folding Mitch's work jeans and communing with the wild-goose wallpaper. "For your information, I *do* know what I can and cannot change. For instance, God has granted me the courage and the wisdom to change this wallpaper."

"O Lord!" teased Mitch above the high whine of the clippers. "Make me an instrument of thy geese!"

"Preach it to the sparrows," I said.

Saint Francis, who had his own haircut problems, would have been proud.

SEVEN

8 Percent Perceptive

On the three-hour car trip across state to Ikea, Mitch was driving and I was filling out a church questionnaire titled "Know Your Spiritual Gifts." The wedding was six months away. It was hard to summon enthusiasm for my role as a bride when I knew that even if I made it on schedule through chemo, mastectomies, and radiation, my hair would have just started to spring up like a crop circle, waving from the scalp like mung beans on the rise. That's a good look for a bride. So far the chemo hadn't made a dent in the tumor. My doctors had tactfully warned me that I might not be "well enough" to pull off an August wedding.

Under the circumstances details about food and dress and service seemed far less urgent than "Know Your Spiritual Gifts." The questionnaire continued for many pages, long and involved, many of the queries redundant and puzzling. I protested most of the multiple-choice options, none of which seemed even remotely close to answers I would have selected. And anyway English majors don't do multiple choice. Scantrons are for slack-

ers! We secretly see multiple-choice tests as cop-outs for con-
formists who can't sustain independent argument. I hadn't
taken a multiple-choice test since the Graduate Record Exam in
1990.

"These answers are silly. And this one contains a comma
splice."

"You think God cares about a comma splice?"

"No," I said. "I'm guessing that God would rather see a
comma splice about Christian service than a correct sentence
about Donald Trump. Though for me it's a toss-up. People
care about grammar even if God doesn't. Grammar may be the
last bastion of institutionalized racism, but a big fat comma
splice in the middle of your spiritual gifts questionnaire sends
the signal that the sponsoring organization doesn't know what
a sentence is."

"So what if they don't?"

"When a document is riddled with grammatical errors, people won't take it seriously."

"If God can forgive the sins of the world, you can get over a
comma splice. Just pick the best answer."

I did so, muttering.

When the analysis arrived in the mail three weeks later—
*GiftQuest Report: Motivating Spiritual Gifts; Identified; Inter-
preted; Applied*—I was pleased to note that the packet contained
graphs and percentages, summaries and injunctions, like a quiz
in *Cosmopolitan*. "Ladies! How Well Can You Satisfy Your Man?
Ten Secrets about Your Butt!"

Ach, I was disappointed in what the report had to say about
my spiritual gifts. There was an 86 percent indication that I had

the gift of Teaching, or Mentoring, and a 72 percent indication of the gift of Administration, or Ruling. "When you function in this, your second gifting," said the *GiftQuest Report* earnestly, "you may be considered like 'shoulders' in the Body of Christ, carrying the load of leadership." No surprise there, except for the misplaced modifier at the end of the sentence. Public speaking and teaching are what I do for a living. However, I noticed that the *GiftQuest Report* was silent on the topic of the gift of Preaching, or what I called Women Claiming Authority in the Church.

The issue of women in church leadership had long been a tender spot for me. It was one of the issues that had propelled me away from my church of origin thirty years earlier. In the early 1980s the American Mennonites were engaging the issue, but their pace was much too slow for me. As a young woman I had zero patience for any group who did not instantly and wholeheartedly affirm inclusivity in both governance and practice. At eighteen I thought it was much more important to be right than loving. Go figure. Now, at forty-eight, I think it is much more important to be loving than right.

Change comes harder to communities than to individuals. My solution to this problem thirty years ago was to ditch the community. This solution, though, throws the baby out with the bath water. When communities begin tackling top-heavy, sticky issues that require tact, pacing, and wisdom, seasoned leaders like my father know not to expect instant change. Yet I was embarrassed that the question of women's leadership in the church was still an issue now in the twenty-first century. The thought made me wince, as when running, you put too much pressure on a once-broken talus. I hated to use words that in intellectual circles had been out of style since the identity politics of the 1980s—*patriarchy, hegemony, misogyny*. But just because we didn't say them didn't mean they weren't still around. Gender was a fissure, a fault line, in contemporary Christian circles. Put too much pressure on it, and something flared up.

At the Christian college where I teach, many of my students have never heard of Lilith. Eve they know. Lilith, not so much. That is, they remember Lilith from *Cheers* reruns. This character was a turbo-bitch played by Bebe Neuwirth. In a sit-com featuring various male goof-ups and losers, Lilith was an uptight professional who busted chops, scared men, and bunned her hair into a locked knob that said, "Dead bolt, Bucko." Her expressionless face had a neutral Pleistocene chill, like a woolly mammoth under ice. Lilith was cold. The implication for alert viewers was that her advanced education had made her so. In other words, female achievement prevented a woman from being warm and loving. The message was "Hahaha, careful, ladies! Don't get too smart on us, or you'll turn yourself into an undesirable ball-buster!"

The *Cheers* Lilith was merely a passing nod, a witty gesture, to the first Lilith, the Lilith of legend and lore. According to the Talmud, Lilith was the first wife of Adam in the Garden of Eden. Too bad she was a monster of selfishness, but what did God expect, having made her from filth? I guess God was fresh out of the nice clean dust he had used to make Adam. Lilith was in touch with her sexuality. Let's just say she had explored her anatomy in a hand mirror. We infer, as Adam must have, that her sexual desire was a metaphor for aegis in decision making.

None of that for Adam! He demanded a position of sexual sub-servience, as if to literalize the power imbalance between them. Perhaps this was the first known occasion for those immortal words, "My way or the highway!" So Lilith ran away to the Red Sea, where she set herself up as her own authority. She began to cavort with demons, defiantly celebrating a variety of sexual positions there in her love shack by the side of the sea.

The folkloric tradition reinforces a useful life lesson. You can't have sex with demons and expect all to be well. Don't sleep with just anybody, for heaven's sake. Because you'll just have to pay the piper if you go to bed with the likes of fallen angels! Lilith embodies the archetype of the unwed mother. She began to breed lots of unwanted half-demon babies called *lilim*. What's a grouchy unwed mother to do? Lilith had a thought: "You know what? I could eat them!" And that's exactly what Lilith did, becoming the first in a long line of Unnatural Mother figures, a monster of literal consumption.

Over the centuries of religious commentary, Lilith has come to represent the dissenting and transgressive woman, the one who has a grudge against God. In order to get revenge on Adam and his next wife, Eve, Lilith snuck back into the Garden of Eden disguised as a serpent. Some folks are surprised by the idea of a female Satan figure, but newsflash: that bad boy can shape-shift. Call him Legion, for he is many! Artistic renderings of a girlie, full-figured Satan appear in the most celebrated churches in Christendom. If you don't believe me, look up Michelangelo's *Temptation and Fall*. This is the super-famous painting in which God is reaching out to touch Adam's finger. Right there at the top of the Sistine Chapel, Satan appears coiled around the

Tree of Life, half snake, half babe. You can't help but notice that Satan is not a he. As Mitch would say, dude looks like a lady. In fact he looks a little like Mae West. Check out his boobs.

Whether or not you grew up with the story of Lilith, you have to admit that the history of Western religion depends on a vision of women that is pretty toxic. Eve may not be eating *her* babies like trail mix, but she's the Mother of Lies, blamed fully and richly for the temptation and fall of man. In fact it is hard to find a biblical woman who *isn't* a nastypants. Do we even know who the good Bible women are? We're all familiar with Mary, Mother of Christ, but how many of us can tell the tales of Miriam, Anna, Huldah, or Deborah? Whereas we can all provide a thumbnail bio on the temptress Eve, the landshark Jezebel, the cheat Rebecca, the vampire Delilah, and the denialmeister Lot's wife.

Paul's New Testament injunction that women should not preach in the church has had invidious staying power, even in church denominations that purport to honor the leadership of women. Knowing what I know of Lilith and Eve and harlots and witches and Mae West, I was not all that surprised when the *GiftQuest Report* discreetly downplayed my gift of teaching. Teaching was the perfect gift if you were a man, maybe. If you were a woman, there was a better gift. For instance, hospitality!

The *GiftQuest Report* urged me to arrange flowers for the Lord. Apparently, as a tertiary gifting, I had Giving, or Hospitality, checking in at a modest 58 percent inclination. The report's example of hospitality was flower arrangement. I chuckled when I read that the Lord had blessed me with the gift of flower arrangement. My mother has been making fancy altar bouquets for her church ever since I was little. Every summer she depletes her rose garden for this cause. It was she who taught me and my sister the value of keeping fresh flowers in the house year-round. Even in Bible School, when she and my father lived in the shabby dormitory for married couples, she always grew a couple of blooming pots so that she could bring those vivid spots of cheer indoors. "When you're sharing a bathroom with two other couples, the world looks much nicer with a few mums on the table," she'd say firmly.

Mennonite women everywhere had a long background in flower arranging, and I suspected that Pentecostal women weren't too far behind. The Pentecostal church we attended was positively fulsome with floral arrangements, the sanctuary festooned with new and delectable creations each Sunday. Busy hands were working long and hard behind the scenes.

But I naturally wondered about *men* and flower arranging. How many of the men of this congregation had been advised that they enjoyed the gift of Giving, or Hospitality? Had *any* hospitable gents been encouraged to arrange flowers for the glory of our Savior? Did the *GiftQuest Report* ever even assign hospitality as a spiritual gift to a man? My Pentecostals were an old-fashioned group. They called the women *ladies*, and they believed that men needed to step up to the plate in the spiritual leadership of their homes. If they were to assign a man the gift of flower arranging, there would have to be a literal biblical precedent. I frowned, trying to think of one. Surely there were hospitable male hosts in the Bible? Abraham's nephew Lot could be considered hospitable, sort of, if you ignore certain creepy disclosures in the Genesis account. It was hard to imagine the

Apostle Peter with the tertiary gifting of hospitality. "Hi, Jesus. I brought you some Gerbera daisies. And an ear."

At ten I took a similar questionnaire in my Mennonite church of origin. At that time I aced the gift of martyrdom. Exotic! I spent many hours poring over seventeenth-century accounts of Anabaptists who had cheerfully died for their faith. If God called me to the stake, I wanted to be ready. Anabaptists, as a group, earned very high marks in journaling, hymn singing, endurance, and iron spikes through the tongue. I particularly savored a woodcut illustration of such a martyr. Perpetually singing the praises of her Lord and Savior, she had declined to recant. Finally the guy in charge ordered the spike. The *Martyrs' Mirror* reported that even after she took the spike to the tongue, she went on singing. Bleeding and singing, singing and bleeding! I could do that!

For several weeks thereafter I attempted to sing "A Mighty Fortress Is Our God" without moving my tongue. My mother, thinking I was making fun of a fine old hymn, sent me to my room without supper. I protested that I wasn't being sacrilegious—just the opposite! But she would have none of it. Then I realized that if indeed I did have the gift of martyrdom, the thing to do would be to remove immediately to my room, demonstrating a martyr's pure humility. This I did, singing around my immobile tongue. And anyway Mom was making *Cotletten*, Mennonite meatballs, for supper. I wouldn't be missing much.

The best part of my *GiftQuest Report* was its matter-of-fact disclosure of a near total absence of the gift of Prophecy, or Perception. Alas, this sad little 8 percent inclination earned me the following encomium: "This is not a strong gift in you. You do not significantly desire to confront and correct what you see as wrong." Too true. But I consoled myself with the thought that at least I was 30 percent merciful. Mercy, even a third of it, is nothing to sneeze at!

The more I thought about the GiftQuest numbers, the more gypped I felt. Hey! Was the *GiftQuest Report* trying to tell me that I had only an 86 percent indication for my profession of choice? My teaching evals were really high! Like the character of the little overachiever Lisa on *The Simpsons*, I was miffed at the thought of earning only a *B*+. Mind you, I didn't believe in assigning numerical percentages to Spiritual Gifts, but if I did, I would have expected at least a 91 percent inclination.

My *B*+ was especially humbling when Mitch showed me the results of his *GiftQuest Report*. He had received a 93 percent indication for Prophecy, or Perception. *He* didn't mind confronting and correcting what he saw as wrong. I thought of the time he had come home from work to find Albert's kitchen a mess, the burner still on, spaghetti sauce everywhere, like a crime scene. Leroy had invaded his grandfather's kitchen and had been careless in the way of teens. But a hot burner in a blind man's kitchen is no small matter.

If I had come across this scene, I would have cleaned up the mess, turned off the burner, and mentioned the oversight to Leroy. Here's how Mitch handled it. After cleaning up the spaghetti sauce and turning off the burner, he marched downstairs and pitched the entire contents of Leroy's room into the ravine out back—sheets, pillows, skateboard, clothes, guitar, amp, all of it. When Leroy, that charming slacker, rolled in hours later and expressed surprise at seeing his most cherished possessions strewn down the hillside, Mitch said, "This is about respect, son. If you don't respect your grandpa, then you will get no respect in this house."

Leroy never left a mess in his grandfather's kitchen again. Clearly Mitch was a man who could confront and correct what he saw as wrong.

Even in daily parenting Mitch offered casual correction, and, strangely—strange to me, anyway—his casual correction was received. Mitch's colloquialisms often threw back, way back before he was born, to the 1950s. I heard him teasing Leroy, who was having a pity party about something. "Billy Boohoo gonna cry or what?" demanded Mitch in his big calm voice. It turned out that Mitch often "Billied" his son. It was Billy This and Billy That. When Leroy would announce halfway to Grand Rapids that he had forgotten his date's wrist corsage in the fridge, Leroy became Billy the Forgetter. Still driving, Mitch straightened an imaginary tie, pretended to ring a doorbell, and said, "Hello Mrs. Morgan's Mom, I'm Billy the Forgetter. I'm unemployed, and I don't have a corsage for your daughter, but I'm lookin fly with my mohawk and skinny pants."

"You can't say Billy the Forgetter," I objected. "There's no alliteration. It needs to be Frank the Forgetter."

"Nah, honey. Billy."

Leroy, in the backseat, surprised me by liking the style of this exchange. "Mrs. Morgan's Mom," he said politely, ringing his own doorbell, "I'm Billy the Forgetter. I got no corsage, and no driver's license, and my forehead is broken out. But I really like your daughter."

Since that time I have also heard Billy No Wipe, Billy Red

Legs, Billy the Oversleeper, Billy Foot Odor, and Billy the Waster of a Perfectly Good Casaba Melon.

I was willing to admit that Mitch might deserve his *A* for successful gift deployment. But I wanted an *A* too. And I was troubled that I wouldn't have a chance to use my gifts in Mitch's church because there were no women in leadership. There were female elders, but always in the capacity of Mrs., women attached to husbands.

Did God want me to use my gifts in the church body? If so, I was pretty sure that the Pentecostals wouldn't want to learn what I had to teach.

Nearing the end of our day trip, as we turned off the highway at Ikea, Mitch asked me the question that changed everything.

"Honey," he said. "What if God ain't callin you to teach in the church? What if he's callin you to learn?"

My heart stuttered into instant humiliation—oh, oh, oh! I wasn't supposed to teach the Pentecostals! They were supposed to teach *me*!

It had never occurred to me that I was missing the largest implications of the huge recent shift in my life. Here was a brand-new church, challenging for me in so many ways. Like the big dummy I often am, I had assumed that altered circumstances meant altered lives. I had assumed that because the external circumstances of my life were so radically different, *I* must be radically different.

But change doesn't work like that. Altered circumstances give us only the *opportunity* to change. *We* actually have to do the work. We have to make the decision to gets things moving, and then we actually have to move them. We can't sit around and wait for other people to do our work for us. We can't even sit around waiting for God to do our work for us. In the new circumstances of my life I had been expecting that all the old things would keep happening. I would teach, they would listen. I would lead, they would follow. I would speak, they would take notes.

There arose in my mind an image, unbidden and unpleasant. One day a guy at Mitch's job didn't show up for work—no call, nothing. Some of the women from personnel got worried and went to Louis's apartment. They tried to get the manager to let them in. He wouldn't. Finally they persuaded the manager to go and check up on him. Turns out Louis had been bitten by a brown recluse, and for three days had ignored the oozy swollen mark on his belly. The manager came back and reported that Louis was comatose on the floor.

When Mitch told me this story, I was stupefied that anyone could have chosen to ignore a swollen, itchy, oozing, obvious spider bite, right at the physical center of the body. Lalala! Not happening, lala! Do nothing, lalala, microwave some popcorn! But now I remembered the recluse story and nodded. The meaning of epiphany is sometimes tardy and retroactive. We don't see it until some time has passed, despite signs, despite pain, despite the blow to the belly. And if we do nothing, we make things worse. If we stray off-topic, we put ourselves in real danger of missing the central thing, the thing the universe wants us to focus on. Once again I had been slow to see the point. Righto, change means *change*! Change means *I have to do something different*!

I swallowed hard. This was a tough lesson. I had been so busy thinking of what gift I could give the people of my church that I had lost sight of the gift God was giving me. Here was another perfect gift. I hadn't asked for it. I didn't even know if I wanted it. But it was a gift that would change my life. God was giving me a chance to shut up and learn.

Hospitable maybe I was, but my adult life had not been characterized by meek silence. From a purely literary perspective, Lilith had been my hero—she who had refused to submit, she who had dismissed and transcended all forms of gendered oppression. Lilith had been strong and defiant, not gentle. I had never even valued gentleness, unless you count an afternoon when I was nine, when I first wept through *Little Women*. In this nineteenth-century tearjerker an angelic child named Beth takes a direct hit from consumption and dies on the couch holding her hanky. All through that afternoon I swore that I too would become gentle and shining, dying very gracefully, perhaps embroidering my own death-clothes with tiny rosebuds.

My work was cut out for me. In that moment when Mitch suggested that God might be calling me to learn rather than teach, I decided to accept the gift that God was giving me. As a rule God knows what we want better than we do, so I was prepared to override my feeling that this might be a gift I didn't want. There were things about Mitch's church that made me uncomfortable, both in teaching and in praxis. It was clear that if I accepted this gift, I would actually have to demonstrate change. My old self would have just ditched Mitch's church and looked for another. My old self would have said, "I want to be comfortable; I want everyone to believe what I believe." But sometimes growth happens best when we accept discomfort and difference.

Here was a holy invitation to learn. From now on, if I disagreed with something I heard from the pulpit, I wouldn't focus on the thing I had a problem with. I would focus instead on what I could take away. Or, better yet, on what I could bring to God. I didn't have piety, or purity, or world-overcoming faith. But there was one thing I could do, and that was pledge not to put my mouth on the man of God, except in prayer.

Don't get me wrong. This decision didn't involve a magical transformation of my core beliefs and values. I still believed that the idea of divine calling transcends the very barriers we use to codify categories of ethnicity, race, gender, and sexual orientation. How could we call it a *divine* calling if it didn't supersede our own human categories? In brief, I believed that any adult man or woman of faith who felt called to serve in a pastoral role should be able to pursue training, ordination, and leadership opportunities.

I knew that my beliefs, which were based on many years of scholarship, were unlikely to change. But I could assign them a different level of importance. Who knew what I would see when I stopped looking for structural and semantic flaws in the organization of this church, indeed of all churches? I thought of the four gorgeous months I had spent as an adult when I had returned to my Mennonite community of origin. As a young woman, I'd seen only the imperfections. As an adult, I'd seen something truly beautiful among these same people. I'd seen that in spite of those same imperfections, my church of origin was alive with love and growth. God works through imperfect people, through imperfect churches, through imperfect faith. Isn't that, after all, the ineluctable beauty of religion?

English professors are trained to limn, contest, and quibble. You should see us at faculty meetings—it's like trying to herd cats. No issue's too major for a soapbox; no issue's too minor for long-winded hairsplitting. Props to my colleagues for their rich intellectual commitments! I mean it. I really do respect them. But I had no desire to model the life of the spirit after the life of the mind. Overinvestment in the life of the mind had brought me neither peace nor joy. I was ready to try something else. I decided to sit very still and see what God would do with this new circumstance.

Lilith and everything she represented—the insistence on voice, on authority—began to fade to a footnote in a blurry font, like a point made in a fussy dissertation. The issue of women in church leadership was and still is very important to me. But it appeared on a page I had already turned, and I needed to keep reading. I knew in my knower that now I needed to shift my focus from whatever was missing to whatever was pure, lovely, virtuous, of good report, and filled with praise.

For starters, I determined to apply the lesson I had learned as Mitch and I renovated our home. What worked in one house could apply to another. The church was also a house, the house of faith. I would focus on what this church had, not on what it didn't have. This decision left me oddly breathless. I had the feeling that I was opening the door on something big, that gigantic wheels had started turning. God was going to show me something—now that I was ready to see it.

EIGHT

ℐ

The Gottman Island
Survival Experience

God was already showing me how a Christian relationship could be different from one not rooted in faith. Mitch and I were getting married in six months, but I naturally spent some time wondering why, if Christian marriage by definition enjoys God's blessing, the divorce rate among Christians is just as high as it is among non-Christians. Something was wonky. I suspected that the wonkiness existed in proportion to the wisdom with which the two people chose each other. Maybe Christians were clinging to the blighted notion that marriage would be easy. Maybe they thought that God would automatically bless them with peace and compatibility just because they were entering into a Christian covenant. If he did, Christians wouldn't be filing for divorce like everybody else. Let's say, though, that you have found a sexy someone, and you feel optimistic about your future together. You feel excited about the possibilities. How, in the face of your fabulous new-relationship chemistry, can you even begin to assess?

The American novelist Peter De Vries once said, "The difficulty of marriage is that we fall in love with a personality, but must live with a character." If I was in love with Mitch's personality at the beginning of the relationship, how would it be possible to proceed with wisdom?

The Gospel of Mark steered me in the right direction. It tells the story of a desperate but fabulous dad, my all-time favorite biblical character. I would set this guy up with my single girl-friends in a heartbeat because, wow, he's honest and direct. He's a risk-taker, too. He has a son who would break any parent's heart. Since babyhood the son has been having big foamy convulsions, trying to throw himself into the fire. Whether you read the boy as a suicidal demoniac or a mute epileptic, it is clear that the loving, long-suffering dad has finally bottomed out over his son's illness. The dad has tried everything, and he doesn't know what to do anymore. So as a last resort he's bringing the problem to Jesus. Curiously, the son's condition isn't the point, even though everybody loves a good demon story.

Rather, the point of the story is the *dad's* condition. He's distressed, he's broken, he's at the end of his rope. When Jesus says that anything is possible for those who believe, the dad cries out, "I do believe; help my unbelief!" I interpret this as, "I'm doing the best I can with faith, but I'm really, really bad at it!" The dad's faith was blocked by years and years of parenting a son who never got any better. Don't we all have something that blocks our faith? Mine has been blocked too, not by a child, but by my mind. In fact I read the tormented child as a metaphor for the tormented mind, possessed, as it were, with a destructive skepticism. I cling so hard to ratiocinative thought that I have trouble releasing myself into the mysteries of God.

Also, sometimes a nice mimosa brunch sounds better than church.

The desperate dad decides that he simply will not let his skepticism stop him from approaching Christ. Sure, the dad has doubts about God. His faith is frail. But he makes a deliberate decision to override his doubts, and to bring his sick boy to Jesus. And Jesus honors that. Jesus heals the boy in spite of the dad's unbelief.

For me the takeaway is that we don't need to be strong and faithful and firm in order to approach God. We can be an unholy mess, like the son, or a frustrated skeptic, like the dad. What a relief it is that we don't have to be good at religion in order to seek God! We don't even have to have a strong sense of belief. All we need is the *desire* to believe.

I decided to approach marriage as the dad approached Jesus. For starters, I needed to take a lesson from this dad and cry out my real feelings. I needed to admit *how good the relationship felt*. I acknowledged and admitted it freely. And then, like the dad, I took a deep breath and set my feeling aside. There was something even more important at stake. I told God that I believed, but I needed him to help my unbelief. I pledged that I would do whatever God wanted me to do. I would even be willing to give up Mitch—because what if I had reverted to my former patterns of denial? What if I was simply so attracted to Mitch that I was *imagining* God's direction in the relationship?

Mitch and I were shooting for a God-centered marriage, the real deal, the kind in which we would literally and symbolically seek God first before any other activity. We wanted the kind of marriage in which we would set our alarm for 5:00 a.m. so that we could pray and meditate in the cool of the day. Mitch was all about seeking God in the cool of the day. Many readers will be appalled by the idea of getting up in the cool of the day, not just on weekdays, but forever. However, I have stopped fighting the inexorable genetic transformation into my mother. Like her, I rise and shine. I bounce out of bed with enthusiastic solutions for global warming. I might like to share a thought about the philosophy of Schopenhauer prior to brushing my teeth. Also, is it not sort of sexy when a big slumbering man is willing to stagger from deep sleep at 5:00 a.m. in order to speak prayerfully about the well-being of his house and family? Mitch even proposed that we renovate a wee sun porch as a room to be set aside exclusively for the cool of the day. I said sure as long as the cool of the day featured a gas heater.

Did a willingness to seek God first make Mitch the man for me? Before I embarked on this spiritual journey, I had dismissed the notion of Christian marriage as faintly ridiculous. Whenever I thought of Christian marriage, I imagined a married pair, let us call them Todd and Pammy, married twenty-two years and conducting middlebrow retreats to freshen Christian romance. Todd and Pammy teach a dynamic, fun-filled seminar bursting with hands-on activities. For instance, couples compete with other couples in a gift-wrapping relay with one hand tied behind their backs. Also, among the many secret envelopes taped to the underside of the conference chairs is one that contains a gift certificate to the Olive Garden. Todd has a PowerPoint that calls attention to dire statistics about Christian divorce—guess what, folks! The people of God have failed at marriage just like regular people! After the break

Pammy transitions to Christian sex, which has highs and lows, seasons and cycles, just like the stock market. "Sex is a beautiful thing before God. God wants you to explore each other's bodies! Oral sex and role-playing can be a part of that Special Intimacy!"

Once I scorned the Todds and Pammys of this world. I wondered if Christian marriage had anything to distinguish it other than Sunday potlucks and wall decals that said in earnest cursive

As for me and my house, we will serve the Lord.

Peering in from the outside, I had always been a cynical observer of the hundreds of Christian marriages in my Mennonite youth. I questioned the love and commitment I saw there. Oh, it was often the real deal. I knew plenty of couples who, like my parents, had lived together in happy monogamy for thirty, forty, fifty years. Two years ago my parents celebrated their fiftieth anniversary. From what I could see as a child, the Mennonite couples around me really did love and honor each other, my folks especially.

What I questioned was how they had come together. My own parents began dating in their early twenties, but they had met for the first time two years earlier, at the Regional Mennonite Brethren Youth Conference. Imagine five hundred upright youth in long modest skirts and pressed serge pants. For entertainment the Conference provided a Bible Show-Down, which the audience met with loud claps and whistles. This was in 1956.

I said to my mother on the phone, "Were the kids in the audience expressing sincere interest? Or were they making fun of the idea of a Bible Show-Down?"

"No, they were excited," she said. "It was exciting."

Each Mennonite church trained its own team of five, and then the church teams went on to compete with other church teams, until you hit the regional level for the final play-offs. My mother and father were stars on their respective teams. I asked my mother what kind of questions they had asked.

"Anything from the book of Acts," she said. "Who was the first female convert in Europe?"

"I give up. Who?"

"Why, Lydia!" Her surprised tone indicated I might be a changeling.

"Right, Lydia. The seller of purple. What else did they ask?"

"Where did the second mission journey originate?"

"That seems kind of nitpicky."

"But I knew the answer!" she said joyfully. "When I jumped up—"

"You didn't have a buzzer or anything?"

"No, when you knew the answer, you had to jump up. When I jumped up, so did your father on his team. It was a tie. They called on him first, but he got it wrong."

"And you got it right?"

"We won the championship. I noticed him noticing me then."

"Did you come home thinking about him?"

"Oh no," she said. "I came home thinking about Waldo and Fonda. Waldo was our youth-group director. He coached us. When we won, he took us all on a trip to the Thousand Islands in the Saint Lawrence River. We saw Boldt Castle. Guess what Waldo did? He was just a gas-station manager, but he paid for us all out of his own pocket! This was before seat belts. We squeezed into his old Buick, four in the back, three in the front. It was a two-hour trip, and I was wedged onto Fonda's lap the whole way there. Fonda made the best rhubarb pie."

"Better than ours?"

"I've been using Fonda's recipe for fifty-some years," she said. "Waldo and Fonda had a big impact on us. All of us kids wanted to have a marriage just like theirs. Their home was so warm and welcoming! Waldo was nervous when he got up in front of the kids to talk, but we loved the way he treated Fonda. Just like a queen."

"Why would anybody be nervous to talk in front of a roomful of kids?"

"He had a nervous tic. He used to stick his right hand in and out of his coat pocket."

"Like a Mennonite Napoleon?"

"Except that he was shy. We called him Horse Bun."

"You called your youth leader Horse Bun?"

"Not to his face! He had a large mole on his hand." My mother chuckled. "It looked like a horse bun."

"Don't you think it was kind of mean to call your beloved youth leader Horse Bun?"

"Oh, we were immature," she explained. "But we sure did know the book of Acts!"

∽

My mother and father were each other's first serious relationship. My father had had exactly one date with another girl, Lena Liebelt, the prettiest girl in the entire community. Over the years, from various Mennonite oldsters including my mother, I have heard stories about Lena Liebelt's otherworldly beauty. However, my father and Lena Liebelt turned out to have nothing in common, besides being Mennonite youths who could shake a tailfeather when quizzed on New Testament trivia. It seems strange to me that an eighteen-year-old boy would have had the wisdom to demote the importance of smokin' hot curvalicious beauty. Yet it must have been so, for my father did not ask beautiful Lena Liebelt for a second date. Fortunately she had plenty of other suitors.

These young men and women were traditional Mennonites from a righteous generation, one that had no knowledge of external cultural events such as the sexual revolution. And anyway this was in the fifties, in a Mennonite settlement far beyond the reach of poodle skirts. Mennonite girls weren't parking and kissing. They were ironing and weeding. If they wanted to be bad, they cut their hair. When I asked my mother if her parents had ever sat her down for The Talk, she laughed heartily. "No! We weren't sheltered, though. We saw calves being born!"

My mother went out one time each with two nice young men, straitlaced Mennonite youths. One of them, Big Jake, formally asked her father if he could court her. In a revolutionary move, this conservative patriarch took a pass on the traditional role of hands-on, meddlesome dad. "Ask her yourself and see if she'll go with you," he invited. Big Jake drove my mother all the way to Toronto to see Handel's *Messiah*.

"Bold move," I commented. "What if you didn't have anything to talk about for the long car ride?"

"Well, we didn't," said Mom. "There wasn't any chemistry. Big Jake was a DP."

"What's a DP?"

"Displaced person. An immigrant. He had just come from one of the Mennonite colonies in South America."

Before I could object to the label, she continued, "And on the way home from Toronto, he didn't even sing!"

"Freak," I said.

"How can anyone hear the 'Hallelujah Chorus' and not sing? I knew as soon as your father sang to me that he was the one."

"Did Dad sing Handel?"

"We were taking a walk in the park and holding hands, and he sang a melodic little song about a pretty rainbow after the rain." Mom sang the first verse over the phone. I joined in. It's really a dear love song. When she was finished, I asked, "Had you ever heard the song before?"

"No. I made him sing it three times in a row, so I could learn it. Then we sang it together as a duet."

So faded Beautiful Lena and Big Jake from the story of their lives. My parents experienced virtually no relational exploration before they married each other. Both my mother and my father committed to their faith in childhood, living it out in a long steady stream all the way to old age, as a river moves ineluctably toward the sea.

They prayed about their attraction to each other. And of

course they felt that God was pairing them up, a divine match, an anointing of souls united in Christ. But herein lay my area of concern. How could they have been mature enough at age twenty-one to know who they were, let alone know what kind of partner would suit them in later decades? God's blessing would have been a great convenience to them, and I believed that they had imagined it. We see this sort of convenient revelation all the time, as when fundamentalist Christians announce that God hates all the same folks they hate, or when your eighteen-year-old son thinks it is God's will that he drop out of high school and go mooch off his friend's mom.

It seemed obvious: my parents' inexperience had propelled them to comply with a principle they hadn't bothered to test. They married early, then settled into the bed of their own making. Sad. How narrow their lives had been! How much pleasure and intimacy and self-knowledge they had forfeited through their naïve rush to the altar!

Oops.

Now that I tardily know something about Christian marriage, I would like to offer a wholehearted apology to Mary and Ed, Roger and LaWanda, Ted and Rosalie, Henry and Mary, Peter and Nancy, and so many others. Marriage is a different game when you partner with someone who believes in a power higher than self. I get that now. The difference shows not just in the matter of goals and values, but in the way the marriage runs from day to day.

❦

Mitch's son, Leroy, is 6'2", shaggy-haired, buff as one of those hieroglyphs of King Tut. Girls love him. Leroy, not King Tut. Although who am I to predict the crushes of the young ladies of Holland, Michigan? If they love Justin Bieber, I feel strongly that they might also love King Tut. Or even Genghis Khan. When I was fourteen, I loved one of the Hardy Boys, and also John Christensen, who grew up to be a Greek Orthodox priest. (Hi, Father!)

When I first started dating Mitch, Leroy was sixteen. He had a pretty homeschooled girlfriend with whom he had already celebrated a one-year dating anniversary. He and Chloe dyed their hair odd colors and ran around wearing dinosaur mittens.

Chloe, along with her five siblings, was homeschooled for religious reasons. Her parents were the kind of Christians whose dearest wish was that the public-school curricula would teach Intelligent Design and enforce mandatory prayer. I have only a hazy idea of what Chloe's mother was teaching her, but I do know that Chloe's mom took a firm position as a Dinosaur Nay-Sayer. Chloe's mom was one of a handful of local conservative Christians who believe that dinosaur fossils undermine the Genesis account of Creation. She takes dinosaur fossils personally.

It occurs to me that Dinosaur Nay-Sayers are not unlike Holocaust Deniers, and I'm thinking that dinosaur nay-saying would make a fine topic for a documentary, especially if you could get Barbara Walters to ask in a hushed voice, "Mrs. Scholten, how did you *feel* when you first heard about the Paleozoic Era?" Crazy though dinosaur nay-saying is, I get it. What I don't get is the dinosaur mittens.

Chloe declared that she would not be attending college, due to the unwholesome presence of Satan in our four-year institutions of higher education. I heard Chloe affirm that at Camp Geneva the summer prior she had witnessed an angel sitting on the movie projector. I'm guessing that the angel was on the lookout for evolution documentaries that might sabotage the faith of the campers.

Together Chloe and Leroy signed an abstinence pledge. They announced this before Mitch and I got engaged. We had nothing to do with their abstinence pact, especially since we were busy having hot sex. Mitch believed in premarital abstinence, but apparently his pants disagreed.

Mitch had commenced sexual activity at fourteen, with an eighth-grade girl named Mimi Ledbetter. Mimi Ledbetter was terrifically popular among the boys at E. E. Fell Junior High. Generously endowed, she wore tube tops to Earth Science until one day Mr. Boersema had enough of the tube tops and sent her home to change. For Mr. Boersema the breaking point— the day on which he simply could not take another tube top stretched over those assertive breasts—occurred about halfway through the semester. Mitch assures me that Mimi Ledbetter had been wearing the tube tops from day one. From Mr. Boersema's anagnoritic disgust we may infer that tube tops produce their effect only in a gradual sort of way, like a time-release cold capsule.

Alas, Mitch could not remember what Mimi Ledbetter was wearing when she returned to class after having gone home to ditch the tube top, but I'd like to think it was a broadcloth shirt with a tremendous gap in between the buttons across the chest.

There was a girl like Mimi Ledbetter in my own junior high, and her buttons were positively chomping at the bit. When Mitch made his first sexual overture to Mimi Ledbetter, she was wearing raccoon eyeliner and Peppermint Kissing Potion. Her skintight Dittos offered a handy under-the-crotch zipper that ran up the back side. This is why I have changed her name. She probably doesn't look back on grade eight as her best year, poor dear.

All this is to say that for many years sex had played a formative role in Mitch's romantic relationships. And the same could be said for me. It was astonishing, then, that we both arrived at the idea of premarital abstinence at the same time.

I have to back up a bit. Long ago, in my early twenties, I rejected Mennonite modesty as a bogus trick calculated to perpetuate women's shame about their libido and/or pubic hair. When female rhesus monkeys are overcome by their hormones, they march right up to the alpha male and stand there helpfully lifting their tails up. If that doesn't do the trick, they slap the ground in front of him, briskly and smartly, as if to say, "Chop-chop, we haven't got all day!" Some women are like that. "You, sir! Yeah, I'm talkin' to YOU!" [Lifts skirt.] "Look what I got!" I may not have been quite so brazen, but I had learned that sexual well-being was like anything else: it required clear communication and forward movement.

So I was mystified at first by Mitch's slow pace. On our first date, the one that established how very little we had in common, he accidentally brushed my thigh. I thought the touch was purposeful, provocative, but Mitch doesn't even remember it. The accidental brush startled me. Sometimes you know from the smallest gesture that you could be pulled in, like a kite.

When Mitch and I began dating in earnest several months later, my recognition of what lay between us—the possibility of a real relationship—was gradual. Mitch says he knew right away that I was The One, a communication whispered to him by a still small voice in the grocery store, where we first spotted one another in the Nut-and-Snack aisle. Hence Mitch was determined to take it slowly from the start. I cannot rule out the still small voice of divine Providence, but as one who never heard it, I would have preferred to initiate hot sex right away. Personally, I felt that the Lord Jesus, who gave us our hot pants in the first place, would understand.

Instead Mitch and I dated for a tantalizing five months before the start-up. One afternoon he finally held my hand in a movie theater. This was during a documentary about a group of altruistic singing senior citizens. I thought a kiss was sure to follow, but no. That night when he brought me home, he walked me to the front porch, hands in his pockets, whistling. "I had fun tonight," he said. "Bye!" On other occasions he brought me flowers; he cooked for me; he read out loud to me; he took me hiking. But still no kiss.

I was starting to wonder if there was a spirit of shame, as when in college my best friend Lola dated a guy whose kissing reluctance turned on a deep-seated embarrassment. This guy of Lola's was unable to kiss without building long bridges of spittle. The kicker was, the bad kisser *knew it*. This man is now a celebrated leader in the Mennonite community. I sometimes see him when I'm in California to visit my folks, and, although he is married with grown-up children, I cannot help remembering Walt Whitman's famous lines every time I see him:

And you, O my Soul, where you stand...
Seeking the spheres, to connect them;
Till the bridge you will need, be form'd—till the ductile anchor
  hold;
Till the gossamer thread you fling, catch somewhere, O my Soul.

When Mitch eventually emailed me a polite request to kiss me on the next date, I asked if he maybe wanted to solicit my father's permission first, like the earnest young man who had courted my mother. Dang. Since when do ex-stoners post notice of intention to kiss?

But the chemistry had been building, and it turns out that the wait gave us a teasing, protracted vision of the passion with which we would eventually connect. I remembered this waiting period later when one of my doctors soberly advised us to cease and desist during chemo.

Any infection, any germ, could tank my fragile immune system. If I couldn't keep my white blood cells up, they'd have to stop the chemo and give me a month or two off. But I didn't have a month or two. This was a voracious T rex of a tumor, running fast on creepy little legs. Abstinence was clearly a good idea. Besides, how sexy could I feel under the pall of constant nausea, the taste of coat hangers lingering in my mouth?

People think that the main beauty challenge of cancer is how to pull off a long flowing silk scarf tied over your baldness. Scarf, schmarf. I'm here to tell you that you wither and drift, gaunt as the lepers who shadowed the tombs in days of yore. By the time you start the Taxol phase, your whole body is producing a sickish-sweet metallic odor, which, if bottled, would be called "Come, Maggots!" I got a good chuckle out of those popular you-go-girl cancer narratives, in which the gritty protagonist wears a different pair of Jimmy Choos to each chemo appointment. Ladies, cancer can be fabulous! For the love of MAC, get in touch with your inner vixen and put on some lip gloss! Show off your weight loss with some snug jodhpurs, perfect for the hospital lobby! At the time Mitch and I began considering abstinence I had six remaining eyebrow hairs, five on one side and a loner on the other, crying in the wilderness like John the Baptist.

Mitch figured that divine grace had equipped him with a special gift. He found it downright easy to support me in all this unpleasantness. Driving me to my endless medical appointments, sitting with me through the long hours of chemo, he'd often remark that he was the perfect man for this job. And although I was physically repellent, he wasn't repelled. He couldn't keep his hands off me. He'd kiss me passionately, iron mouth or no. "You're my hot bald fiancée," he'd say, running his hand down my emaciated form.

I looked like a Lincoln log. I raised a former eyebrow.

"Honey, you look bald *on purpose.*"

The more I thought about it the wiser abstinence seemed. But I was reluctant to tell Mitch. I'm a little uneasy about the idea of withholding sex. The idea of withholding sex has historically been attached to feminine manipulation. So often the withholding of sex, like the tyranny of illness, is a bid for power or attention, the passive-aggressive weapon of women who have not learned to communicate their wants and needs.

I decided to tell Mitch that I wanted to try abstinence purely for health reasons. Moreover, I'd try to bring it up on our very next date. This date would consist of reading aloud to each other from lame self-help marriage manuals. Our plan was to do all the exercises at each chapter's end, no matter how ridiculous. The marriage manuals were about developing moral character, so I tried very hard to take them seriously.

Tragically, the marriage manuals we ordered weren't very smart. At points, moreover, they were so lame that they provided excellent material for conversations with my sister. "Speaking of freshening up your marriage," said Hannah at the close of one such call, "Christine and her husband invited me and Phil to go hear the Reverend Lloyd Ogilvie give a talk on marriage."

"I've never heard of the Reverend Lloyd Ogilvie."

"Me neither, but he's written, like, fifty-two books. He was Senate chaplain in the late nineties. I checked out his website. I heard a rumor that he thinks the Antichrist is Eckhart Tolle."

"Hah. Good one." Tolle is a spiritual teacher who focuses on a call to peaceful presence, consciousness, and spiritual growth. "No disrespect to the Reverend Lloyd Ogilvie, but I thought Ann Coulter was the Antichrist."

"Do you remember in junior high when everybody thought Spiro Agnew was the Antichrist?"

"That wasn't Spiro Agnew. That was Henry Kissinger," I said. "He won the Nobel Peace Prize. Which probably wouldn't stop him if he wants to go on from there to become the Antichrist."

"The Nobel Peace Prize might even give an aspiring Antichrist a leg up."

"I'm thinking that this would be a nice ice-breaker at a party—who are your top ten candidates for Antichrist?"

"The Olsen twins," my sister suggested.

"The petite professor at Olivet who called me a Large Poet."

"She called you a *what*?"

"He. He called me a Large Poet."

"You've got to be kidding."

"No, I swear. I was coming out of the elevator and this super-tiny man in a bowtie stops me and says, 'You must be the Large Poet I've been hearing about.'"

"Excuse me, but you're shaped like a chive. You're tall, not large! Why couldn't this annoying little midge see the difference?"

"Because he was the Antichrist, that's why!"

"I bet this professor had a crease ironed down the front of his pants."

"As predicted in Revelation."

My sister and I discussed an online Antichrist survey, and then an Antichrist coffee-table book with celebrity endorsements and glossy photography. Surely such a publication would make a thoughtful hostess gift! And could an Antichrist reality show be far behind?

Try as I might, I still couldn't broach the abstinence issue to Mitch. Meanwhile there remained the question of premarital counseling. While we loved our regular church home, our own pastor had an unusual policy. He refused to marry any couple who had been engaged less than a full year. Given the seriousness of my cancer, Mitch and I knew that we might not have a year. We wanted to get married as soon as my doctors okayed me to travel. So we hemmed and hawed and weighed our options, finally deciding to ask the female half of a pastoral couple to marry and counsel us.

Pastor Deanna was white. Her husband was black. Together they pastored a diverse, dynamic little church in which a group of African-American crooners sang backup. Mitch knew some folks there, and we dropped by the service from time to time. Early in my diagnosis, Pastor Deanna, herself a cancer survivor, had contributed the single most useful piece of advice I heard: "Rhoda, here's what all cancer people need to do. Say *I am healed* at least a hundred times a day. No matter what anyone says to you, just smile and say *I am healed*."

I asked, "What do you do when your oncologist presents some unarguable medical development, such as the fact that your cancer has already metastasized to your lymph nodes?"

"That's easy," said Pastor Deanna. "Just smile politely and say, *I don't receive it*."

I imagined myself waving away my oncologist's report like an unwanted cookie. *No thanks, I think I'll pass on that.*

When we went to our first counseling session with Pastor Deanna, I didn't know what to expect. But I knew all bets were off when Pastor Deanna ushered us into her office, handed us each a water bottle, and said, "First of all, I think you two should purchase a juicer. I recommend the Jack LaLanne juicer at Costco. It's only $90, and it really does a job on beets and celery and whatnot."

"I thought Jack LaLanne was dead," I said.

"Not quite," she answered firmly. "He's, like, ninety-five. And his juicer is exactly what you need as you begin your new life together."

With such an auspicious beginning how could I not surrender to the counseling process? The juicer really did do a job on beets and celery. And whatnot. I knew that I would be helpless before this woman.

My spirit of acquiescence transferred to the stack of marriage manuals that lay on Mitch's coffee table.

On our previous date, the marriage manual had advised us to play something called the Gottman Island Survival Game, in which we had to reach consensus on which ten items we would select for a sojourn on a deserted Caribbean island. I perked right up when I read the directions for the Gottman Island Survival Game. Who doesn't love a good list?

We had twenty-six items to choose from. It took about a minute and a half to pick our ten things. Afterward we took a quiz on the Gottman Island Survival experience. "Did you sulk or withdraw? Did your partner sulk or withdraw?" asked the author, presumably Gottman.

"Why would anyone sulk or withdraw?" I asked, mystified. "It's a *game*."

"Maybe Gottman got a little sulky when he tried it out on his wife."

"What makes you think it was a guy who dreamed this quiz up? Maybe it was *Mrs.* Gottman who got sulky. And withdrew."

"Do you ever get sulky and withdraw?" Mitch asked, nobly trying to stay on-topic.

"No. You?"

"No."

We finished the quiz, which encouraged us to explore our irritability and anger. "I'm feeling a little irritated at Gottman," I said. "But I'm willing to talk about it."

"I don't get it. Why would you fight about what to take to a desert island? You're tryin to survive. It's obvious, ain't it? Water, food, a gun! What kind of an idiot would take the fifth of whiskey?"

"The kind who sulks and withdraws."

"I think I'm done explorin my feelings for tonight."

"That's okay. We can explore our feelings again next Saturday. How does that make you feel?"

"Sulky and withdrawn."

At our next session I summoned my courage and announced, "I have something I want to run by you."

We were sitting on his couch, preparing to read a chapter on Christian sex, but from a different book. This was a manual co-written by a couple who had been happily partnered for twenty-nine years. I had naturally read ahead. Anal sex, no; French maid outfits, okay!

Mitch took a deep breath. "I have something to talk about too. Let me go first, because you might not like it."

"Go."

He paused as he always did whenever something weighty was on his mind. "I think God is callin us to be abstinent."

Ah.

After my spooky little chill had passed, we reasoned it out. If sexual restraint had been good for us in the earliest phase of our relationship, what might it teach us now? And there were other reasons that made it seem wise. We wouldn't have to sneak around in Mitch's house, which he shared with his father and son. Albert, blind and extremely hard-of-hearing, would never need to know that we were having sex, but he didn't believe in sex outside of marriage. Neither did Leroy, in front of whom we wanted to set a consistent example. Abstinence would give us a way to respect Albert's values, and a way to parent with integrity. And finally, it might help us on our spiritual journey. Had it not helped centuries of mystics and spiritual teachers who had gone before?

I had never taken abstinence seriously as a biblical commandment. To me it had seemed about as relevant as killing a fatted calf. In ancient cultures they needed to safeguard patrimony, but modern times, with DNA testing, birth control, and the delay between puberty and marriage, were different.

Like so many others of my generation, I extracted a principle and discarded the rest. The central idea was to treat sex with seriousness, with monogamy. Sleep with one person at a time. Don't have sex without love. Don't have a stiff vodka martini when your cat dies, don't phone a colleague, and don't accidentally have sex with him. In other words, it had never even occurred to me that the Bible might fruitfully be read—at times—in a literal sense. In the sense of, "Hey folks, keep it in your pants until you're married."

Nor had it occurred to me that premarital chastity could be a good thing. I had always thought of it as the ultimate repressive gesture of organized religion on its worst behavior. It seemed a privation dreamed up by ego-driven fanatics intent on shaming and judging a perfectly natural function of the human body. By defining the rest of humanity as whores and fornicators, abstainers gave their egos a sanctimonious boost. Sexual shame is the perfect little stepladder to self-righteousness.

"Let's see what happens when we give up sex on purpose, for the glory of God," I said. I actually heard myself uttering these words.

"And for the good of chemo."

"We should have some sort of ceremony to mark this moment of forfeiture."

He made a noise like "Pfffffttttt!" and leaned over to kiss my one remaining eyebrow hair.

As we all know, college students are horrified when forced to acknowledge that middle-aged people have sex. Tragically, they don't know that the sex they themselves are having is bad, very bad, while midlife sex rests on thirty years of practice. One of my maternal aunts once mentioned that on a group Mennonite vacation to Puerto Vallarta, the wives had all shared one hotel room, and the men, another. It sounded like a slumber party for oldsters. Why would any partnered couple go on a romantic getaway and then not sleep together? When people say, "We got away to the coast for a little R & R," I have always understood them to mean "We had great sex followed by some tasty ahi with mango salsa." Surprise at the separate hotel rooms must have shown on my face, because my aunt said, "When you get to be our age, you don't need to spend every night in the same bed." *That will never be me*, I thought. Which is to say that although I am middle-aged, sex is important to me. Extremely important.

Here is what we learned during our eight months' season of waiting. When something is taken away, you begin to focus on what remains. We have only two choices when an important thing disappears from our lives: either we resent what is missing, or we accept the loss. Either we look at what we don't have, or we look at what we do have. The choice is ours. When Mitch and I began to redirect our sexual energies to what remained, our relationship deepened and broadened. It became a thing of wonder to me. How could it be? The math didn't compute. Ordinarily when something is subtracted, less remains. But in this case more remained. And this thing that I call "more" began to proliferate and grow. It steadied us, it enriched us. We traded eight months of sex for some pretty amazing things: rock-solid commitment, knowledge of character, patience, a new intimacy that made our old relationship seem jejune.

And our season of abstinence showed us something that we might not have otherwise seen. We learned directly, experientially, that both of us had misused sex in the past, and that our vision of sex had been blocking our spiritual growth. It's not that we had overvalued sex. It's that we had been using it as a substitute for real intimacy.

I had never contested a popular notion that one encounters everywhere in American culture, especially in media directed to women—namely, if you don't have sex at least once a week, your relationship will suffer. The negative effect is supposedly invidious, gradual. You and your partner begin to get a little snippy. You begin to pick little fights. You feel distant rather than connected. You fall asleep with the TV on.

In previous relationships I had often noted the truth of this observation. Good sex was good glue. It kept couples tight. I had therefore gone out of my way to prioritize sex—in focus, in frequency, in everything. And in all those years I never considered the possibility that I was *misusing* the gift of sex. I was asking it to do the work of intimacy for me.

It wasn't until I tried abstinence that I arrived at a useful conclusion. Sex should enhance intimacy, not replace it. This is because sex is a pretty pale substitute for intimacy, even when you're crazy hot for your lover. Abstinent, Mitch and I were forced not only to build real relational intimacy, but to understand how very much we had underestimated the potential and richness of sex.

Mitch and I sailed into our wedding with hearts buoyed by gratitude. In spite of our catastrophic decision making in the past, we were marveling at this reprieve, this second chance at happiness. For most of my chemo, my tumor was nonresponsive. This meant that I wouldn't make it, as the cancer mass was too large to be operable. Moreover, because the cancer had already traveled to the lymph nodes, all signs pointed to further cancer, in my case probably the brain, liver, bones, or lungs.

Physically healthy people do not usually expect an early death sentence. Yet I was strangely okay with it. What choice did

I have? Only the choice of my attitude. Unlike many who had died young, I would have a chance to tell my friends how much they meant to me. I would be able to say good-bye. All through that queasy season a tranquility lay around my shoulders, delicate as a pashmina. It became clear that prayer really did make a difference. If I hadn't surrendered to divine will, I would have been fretful, maybe even angry. But it wasn't like that. It was a season of full, rich presence, of mindfulness in the moment, even as the moments ran out. The peace in my spirit was so powerful that I was never afraid. I began to give away art, shoes, jewelry. I made a will and set up a trust. Prayer had become so empowering and so spiritually healing that I no longer worried about physical healing. When I thought of my old life, shut off from God, I knew I'd rather have cancer with faith than health with denial.

Then the tumor suddenly disappeared. It up and vanished a week after an MRI had confirmed its robust presence. The next round of tests revealed it to be 99 percent gone. The remaining 1 percent got axed off the chest wall during my mastectomies a month later. By the time I began radiation, I was in full remission.

After having spent every last cent of our emotional energy on the one-way trip through the cancer tunnel, Mitch and I were expecting nothing but intense relief on our wedding day. On the way to the church the mood was fey. We went through the drive-through window at Starbucks, dressed in our nuptial best. Leroy, joking with us from the backseat, was secretly taking videos of all our nonsense and laughter. (I'm so glad we have those now!) We got the Starbucks girl to lean out of the drive-through window and photograph the three of us. For a wedding-day surprise Leroy had bleached his hair punk-white, like Billy Idol. Mitch and I were singing, "It's a wh-wh-wh-white wedding!"

Now we had made it to that final stretch, the aisle before the altar. Both of us had walked this aisle before; both had stood in other churches with other partners in front of the altar to exchange vows. Nothing had happened during the previous ceremonies to make us anticipate anything other than a spirit of celebration. As we posed for wedding pictures, I pretended that I was a lovely bride. What I lacked in hair I made up in happiness. We floated lightly into the church.

Then something weird happened. In the middle of the ceremony, a big somber velvety feeling came down like a ton of bricks. One moment we were merry at heart; the next, wham. It was like an avalanche of sobriety bowing our heads, our necks too frail to support the weight. Standing in front of the altar, I shot my groom a quick stunned glance to see if he too felt the shift. He did; he was as floored as I was. Whoa. We saw at once that it didn't have anything to do with Pastor Deanna. She was delivering a beautiful meditation, saying just what a pastor ought to say.

At first the big solemn feeling seemed amazingly off-topic. But then I suddenly got it. It pointed to fierce covenant and scary sacrament, as if God were keen on showing us just how serious a covenant marriage is. I must have looked as if I had just encountered a burning bush, because Leroy, who was snapping pictures, stopped and gave me a shrug that said, "Dude, your mouth is open." It's not that I suddenly had cold feet. I didn't. But dang, that was some heavy weirdness. Mitch told me later that he felt it at precisely the same moment. We talked of nothing else that day, even though there was some excellent video footage of Leroy making the cat perform "She's a Brick House, Ow!"

The cat was wearing a handsome striped cravat. He cleans up nice.

The solemn feeling lingered all the way through our honeymoon. We hadn't planned the usual romantic getaway. Since my frontal topography looked like the Dakota badlands, we had to let go of our dream of a tropical siesta under a slow fan. In fact we had to eliminate any locale that might invite a swimsuit or a sundress. What kind of resort destination did that leave for our honeymoon? Perhaps my sister's vacation home in woodsy Central Oregon, with its many paved bike paths and its clubhouse featuring taxidermy heads?

Sure!

Hannah's vacation community is a highly groomed, severely Caucasian resort in the piney highlands. On a visit prior to my honeymoon, my mother, sister, niece Allie (then eleven), and I were approaching the pool clubhouse, waiting in line so that the attendant could check our credentials. I spied a list of house rules that spoke to every imaginable situation regarding pool etiquette. The first stipulation on the list was, PERSONS WHO HAVE DIARRHEA SHALL NOT SWIM IN THE POOL.

This rule naturally made me turn to my niece, crook my pinky over an imaginary cup of tea, and murmur in a fake British accent, "My Deah, oh rilllly! Some irregulah youth with diarrhEEEEa has been defecating in the pool!"

My niece didn't miss a beat. "Cheerio, old sport, 'twas I! But I've got that diarrhEEEa problem licked, what ho!"

My sister frowned at me. She must have intuited that my niece and I would affect this Queen Mum accent for the rest of the vacation. "There will be no licking of diarrhea problems in this family," Hannah said. "Honestly, Rhoda, you're as bad as Allie."

"My Deah," I said earnestly, "it is she, not I, who has the diarrhEEEa!"

We had advanced in the line to the clubhouse window. "Does your daughter have diarrhea?" asked the attendant suspiciously.

Allie and I shook with silent laughter.

"No!" said my sister, exasperated. "Nobody in this family has diarrhea!"

"Because if she does, she's not allowed in the pool."

Allie curtseyed to the woman and said, "Quite."

The hushed affluence of this area is so marked that you'd think everyone in the world drove a Lexus and ate nasturtium-lavender sorbet. Hannah and Phil had a private, spacious Jacuzzi under the pines. When I asked my reconstruction surgeon if I would be Jacuzzi-ready by August 18, she said, "By all means. As long as you don't expect to look good. And as long as you don't have open sores from the radiation."

My father had not yet met Mitch, and so my parents boldly suggested that they drive the thousand miles from Fresno to join us for the first few nights of our honeymoon. You may exclaim,

"They did NOT!" Ah, but they did! I hastily add that when they first suggested crashing our honeymoon, we gave them every encouragement known to man. How many newlyweds get to honeymoon with senior Mennonite parents? Mitch and I liked the idea so much that we asked Hannah and Phil and Allie to join us, too. We all smashed enthusiastically into my sister's elegant little cabin. Our first meal together was an enormous Mennonite sausage that my mother had conveyed in an ice chest from Reedley, California. On arrival, she busied herself in the kitchen, serving the sausage with kidney beans in a flavorful onion gravy.

My family members cleared out after a couple of days, leaving us to piney privacy. But even then the honeymoon was odd. The big weird holy feeling stayed with us. It underscored everything we did. We talked about it incessantly, wondering if other couples had felt anything similar. The piney highlands of Oregon feature gorgeous prehistoric rock formations and plenty of remains from the Mesozoic era. Naturally we wanted to investigate the tiny fossilized camels that roamed the region during the Ice Age, because what says "You and me forever, baby," like a tiny fossilized camel? But we couldn't even admire the tiny Ice Age camels without mentioning that we were now united for real, two people in holy, terrifying covenant before God.

After our eight months of abstinence, the sex was electrifying, better than it had ever been. This wasn't just pent-up libido, I tell you. On our honeymoon all movement for me was slow and ginger. The first stage of the breast reconstruction, a two-year process, had left me with tissue expanders rigid as Mt. Rushmore. Scars crossed to and fro, like busy pedestrians. My right fake breast, tough from radiation, was the color of an eggplant. The expanders hurt so much I had to sleep in a corpse pose. How is it possible to look and feel like this and have the kind of sex that we had?

Blessing can be a very literal thing.

NINE

Up from the Deep

When I was a kid, I pulled toward the figurative rather than the literal. It was obvious to me, for instance, that the biblical story of Jonah wasn't about a man and a fish. In this Old Testament story God shoulder-taps Jonah to go preach to the wicked sinners of Ninevah. The folks of Ninevah were apparently partying like it was 1999. But Jonah was, like, "Ninevah? Let me get back to you on that." Maybe he was not the missionary type. Thinking to run away from God, he bought a passage on a ship bound for a distant city, Tarshish. This didn't fly with the Almighty. God sent a big storm to rock the boat. Cue music: *If not for the courage of a faithful crew, the Minnow would be lost!* While the crew was chucking the cargo overboard to lighten the load, Jonah was down in the hold, taking a soothing siesta. As a child I loved this part of the story. Jonah had the avoidance thing down cold, which made him a deeply sympathetic character to me. I too was anxious to avoid a career of mission work.

The shipmaster woke Jonah up, saying, "What meanest

thou, O sleeper? Arise, call upon thy God!" The crew decided to cast lots to see who had jinxed the voyage. Jonah was busted. He finally admitted that yes, he had been trying to flee from the presence of the Lord. Penitent, he suggested that the sailors chuck him overboard, since the storm was all his fault. They did so. Along came a big fish, up from the deep, to swallow him whole. He remained in the belly of the fish for three days, until the thing finally vomited him out onshore. Then he picked himself up, brushed himself off, and dragged his sorry ass to Ninevah.

Now, as a child I believed in men, and I believed in fish, but it seemed clear to me that this story was intended to frame larger concepts. The fish represented the stern hand of a salvific God. A Johnny-on-the-spot leviathan was an obvious allegory. God would save and redirect us, even when we were disobedient chowderheads! The lesson seemed perfectly lucid, even to a child with an overactive imagination. When God wants you to go to Ninevah, you don't run away to Tarshish. When God puts a specific calling on your life, you can't clap your hands over your ears and pretend it's not happening. (That is, you can. I did it myself. But denial isn't God's "A Plan" for anybody's life.)

Trained on Bible stories, I detected an allegorical subtext in all my reading material, a subtext that made the question of literal veracity sort of pointless. Therefore I wasn't asking, "Did this really happen?" I was asking, "What does this mean?"

When Mitch and I first got together, we had dinner with a nice Christian couple who referenced the Jonah story in casual conversation. The husband and wife were citing the story as a metaphor, telling us of a time when they had been reluctant to answer God's call in a matter of service to their church. Something in their tone lay submerged under the current of general conversation. It pressed up from the deep and into my mouth. "Hey," I said brightly, "do you guys believe in the literality of the Jonah story?" An uneasy silence descended—you'd have thought I had asked how much their new couch cost, or what they thought about Obama.

I instantly realized the severity of my faux pas. Apparently, in Christian circles, unlike academic circles, one did not discuss where literality leaves off and metaphor begins. The wife set down her fork and looked at her husband, who nodded faintly. "We do believe that a big fish swallowed Jonah whole," she said to me gently. She chose her words with clipped care, as if she had just discovered that she was dining with a heretic who deserved a good stoning.

"Speaking of fish," I said into the silence, "this trout is delicious. Is there a hint of saffron in the sauce?"

Mitch has made me understand why some people privilege the literal. It's not that he can't see the figurative. He gets it. He just doesn't *like* it. Figurative readings, according to him, are partial interpretations that often lead the reader off-topic, away from the most meaningful point. In general, he thinks the language of configuration—synecdoche, metonymy, anthropomorphism—is unnecessarily peripatetic. "Just say what you mean. Ain't no call for roundabout poetic language."

I very much enjoyed the way Mitch processed poetry. Once over lunch at Pereddies he and I were talking about how some women seem magnetically pulled to men who abuse them.

Mitch said, "Women seem prone to enablin. Course there's no shortage of brutes to take advantage of 'em."

"'*The brute brute heart of a brute like you,*'" I quoted.

"That from a poem?"

I nodded. "It's called 'Daddy,' by Sylvia Plath. It's one of the most frequently taught poems in American colleges and universities. It's in practically every anthology. Pretty much every college student has to read it. Listen to the opening lines:

> You do not do, you do not do
> Any more, black shoe
> In which I have lived like a foot
> For thirty years, poor and white,
> Barely daring to breathe or Achoo.

Mitch looked nonplussed, so I added, "The poem has a super-famous last line. The speaker's pissed at her father and she finishes by saying, '*Daddy, daddy, you bastard, I'm through!*'" I did my best Plath imitation.

"I don't get it," said Mitch. "What's so special about hatin your dad?"

"It's a controversial poem. She compares her father to a Nazi. She suggests that her own misery was like the suffering of six million Jews. That's pretty potent stuff."

In response Mitch delicately lifted his thumb and forefinger to his ear and rubbed them together, a gesture I had never seen him make.

"What does that mean?" I asked.

"This is a tiny violin, sugar. It's playin a real sad song. Poor me! Poor me! Pour me another drink! Tell you what. That lady just needs to get over herself."

I laughed so hard I nearly snorted my coffee. "I'm quoting you the next time I teach that poem," I warned.

"Go right ahead. Famous or not, any thirty-year-old lady that still hates her daddy pretty much deserves to stew in her own juices. Why don't she just work it out already? Leave that baggage behind! Maybe she'd get a better handle on things if she started volunteerin down at the homeless shelter."

"She killed herself by sticking her head in the oven in 1963," I said.

"Oh." He meditatively picked up the check and stared without seeing it.

"That poem 'Daddy' is her best piece, you say?"

"Certainly it's her most famous."

"Too bad she died without doin anything useful. How would you like to be known for all time as the lady that hated her daddy?"

"I wouldn't," I said decidedly. "But some folks might disagree with you about her having achieved something useful. She's often considered one of the greatest American poets of the twentieth century."

He slapped down his MasterCard. "Well, folks can praise her to the skies, but it sounds like she was still just a bitter, unhappy lady stuck in the past." He said this with an air of finality, as if the subject were closed.

But then he added, "I gotta say that gassin yourself seems a fair shortsighted way to take care of business. Carbon monoxide don't even work half the time. No offense, but that's a chick thing to do. If you gotta take yourself out, do it with a gun, clean and quick."

"I'll pass that along to my students," I said.

He grinned at me. "Anytime you want me to come and share with your class, you just say the word."

Oh, he'd share, all right! I could well believe that he would notice a text's offbeat details that others might miss. Just the day before, he and I had visited an art gallery. As we descended the stairs into an inspiring old warehouse space, we both got that telltale delicious gleam in our eyes. This is the same gleam that animates even the most jaded art collector when she sees something witty, original, commanding. "Wow!" I exclaimed, staring at a fantastic abstract welded sculpture on the opposite wall. "Look at that!"

He made a beeline for the sculpture. But when he got there, he crouched down and examined the wall beneath the sculpture. "Check out this outlet," he said admiringly. "I haven't seen one of these old ones since I worked at Johnson Controls! This here outlet's old school!"

That was my new favorite art gallery moment. And I suspected that now I'd never again teach Plath without imagining her in an apron down at the homeless shelter.

Mitch's and my relationship continually pitted his literality against my metaphoric imagination. Our personalities, our career choices, and especially our spiritual experiences had been shaped by this selfsame divide, and we would have been fools not to see the ramifications of such a fundamental division. This was a man who affirmed the existence of heaven and hell as actual places that you could go to, like the farmers' market or

Craig's Cruisers. Mitch ruled out the possibility that heaven and hell might merely represent states of human consciousness—that is, he rejected the idea that they might be symbolic shorthand for enlightenment and solipsism, the best and worst that humans can achieve.

I didn't get his rejection. Why do we even need to decide on the status of heaven and hell, since anything we say is mere speculation? Why can't we allow for both the literal and the figurative? Personally, I didn't rule out the idea that heaven and hell might be literal places. Why would I? Maybe they are. I've never been dead.

Of course Jesus *is* a historical figure whose existence has been confirmed by contemporaneous secular historians. I may be on the if about Jonah, but I believe in Jesus. Did Jesus, like Jonah, lie in the belly of the grave for three days before being raised up miraculously for more of God's good work? In other words, was Jesus the Son of God, both human and divine, sent to suffer for the sins of the world?

As a child I pitied anyone who thought otherwise. The Bible is full of people raised from the dead—Jesus, Dorcas, Eutychus, the widow of Zarephath's son, Jairus' daughter, Lazarus, and others. I loved all these stories, especially the one in which Jesus tardily raises up a dear friend from the grave. In this story Jesus arrives at the home of his sick friend Lazarus too late. His buddy has been buried for four days. Jesus is not fazed for a second. "Roll away the stone," he says. The family and friends of Lazarus don't want to do that because, in the words of the King James Version, "He stinketh." As a child I naturally repeated this powerful locution as often as circumstance allowed. One could apply it to brothers, borscht, and roadkill. "He stinketh," I intoned solemnly, whenever I found a squashed toad or a decaying squirrel.

With the biblical example of Lazarus before me, I honored my dead with a Christian burial. The snug plastic box that the Authors cards came in made a serviceable coffin for recently deceased toads, katydids, chicks, and field mice. I lined the box with rose petals, toilet paper, and/or Cheerios. The Lazarus surrogate I laid gently on top, folding in the crispy legs and splayed toes if they did not fit. Black thread sealed the box. It was satisfying to name the dead after classmates one didn't like, such as Crispin Hernandez, who brought his ant farm to school but wouldn't let anybody look at it. Commending Crispin's soul to heaven, I interred the coffin in the orchard. Four days later I'd dig up the box, more theatrical than hopeful. Before breaking the seal, I'd command in a loud clear voice, "Crispin Hernandez, come out, I say!" Afterward I'd dump the corpse, wipe the ick, and replace the card deck for future use. Verily, those Author cards did stinketh. This is why I still associate the nineteenth-century author Henry Wadsworth Longfellow with the smell of toady putrefaction.

In those days I had what I would describe as a simple belief regarding the relationship between Jesus and human deliquescence. I would say that my belief was simple because it had not yet occurred to me to look for other ways of reading the story. Most Christians I know, Mitch included, class the Lazarus account as a miracle.

And so it is, whether you read the story as a literal or figurative call to new life. If Lazarus was peacefully rotting there in the tomb and if at the sound of Jesus' voice, he up and trotted out—well, miraculous! He left death and disease behind, yay! Stank hath no hold on him! But we can also read the story another way. In a manner of speaking, are we not dead before we hear the call to rise up and leave behind the things of the grave such as self-absorption, denial, bitterness, and blame? And when we respond to the call of Christ, do we not begin to live anew? We leave the old life behind even as Lazarus leaves behind his stink, his tomb, and the sickness that killed him. A changed life in Christ is undoubtedly a miracle, as anyone who undergoes such change will attest. I tried for twenty-five years to change on my own and couldn't. And now I have finally, belatedly, experienced change through grace. Which resurrection is more miraculous?

Dating Mitch prompted me to attend church regularly, but spiritual change had been creeping up on me for some time. It started five years ago, when after a long absence I went back to visit the Mennonite community in which I'd been raised. Elsewhere I've written about what I saw there, but I haven't written about what I took away. In simple terms, I saw that people who live by the Spirit experience the Fruits of the Spirit. In the New Testament book of Galatians the Apostle Paul promises believers that the life of faith yields good and practical fruit: love, joy, peace, long-suffering, kindness, goodness, faithfulness, gentleness, and self-control. Who wouldn't want those things? I did. Of the nine, I could then lay claim only to two, love and self-control. I adored my family and friends. But isn't it easy to be loving to folks you like? As for self-control, it's no great achievement to run six miles a day when you have a genetic drive to do so. The remaining Fruits of the Spirit were distinctly absent in my life. In fact I was static, restless, impatient, grudge holding, skeptical, and petty. The choices I'd made hadn't made me happy, so I was ready to try something new.

In these past five years my life has changed tremendously. I've had ample opportunity to watch and ward, to look for the Fruits of the Spirit in my own life and the lives of those around me. I still struggle with skepticism, but I've made real progress in the other areas. And I love it that the mystery of faith turns on what is after all a simple logical equation. In surrendering to the divine, we yield to divine transformation. *A* causes *B*. This surrender is the only intentional gesture we can make to invite real and permanent character change. It may not perfect us, but, thank God, it sure makes us better than we were.

When Leroy's dad and I first got married, Leroy was enrolled in remediated classes at the local high school. He was experiencing the joys of reading for the first time in his life. Previously he had thought that reading was something that only grown-ups did, like saving receipts or power washing the house. Mitch didn't read fiction, so every afternoon when Leroy got home from school, he sought me out with bulletins from his grade-eleven American literature class. "Rhoda! Have you read John Steinbeck's *Of Mice and Men*? The character of Lenny is so cool! I rewrote the ending so that he steals an amp and learns how to play bass!" Then, before I could respond, he'd confide, "I decided I was sick of green hair, so Chloe dyed it white again. But she left the dye on too long and the top got sort of pink. I told her that we could say it was in support of breast cancer awareness."

All my life I've been a huge supporter of cleaning things up. It always seemed utterly obvious, for instance, that in order to heal after a breakup, you needed to box all the photos and gifts of the former beloved and get them out of the house.

Not long after Mitch and I were married, Leroy set sail on heartbreak's stormy seas. He came into the kitchen where I was starting dinner, microwaved himself some frozen Jose Olé tacos, and sat down at the bar to review the abject details.

"I just got dumped," he said glumly. "Chloe doesn't think I'm a hard worker. She doesn't think I'm enough of a go-getter. Because I don't have a job."

It seemed like an odd reason to dump someone at seventeen, but who understands the cruelties of youth?

"How did she break it to you?" I asked Leroy.

"It was Brad." Brad was Chloe's father. "It was Brad who told me how Chloe feels."

I set down my knife and paused in the chopping of jicama. "Your girlfriend's *dad* is dumping you?"

He nodded. From his back pocket he removed a small sock monkey, set it on the counter, and stared at it. I inferred that this sock monkey had played a key role in the Catherine wheel of love.

Well, there was only one thing to do, and I did it. I went over and hugged Leroy. But what I wanted to do was suggest that he and I go get a bucket of primer and begin to white out the expressions of love he had written on the walls of his bedroom.

When Mitch and I were hard at work renovating the basement, we invited Leroy to express his own creativity by painting the walls of his bedroom the color or colors of his choice. Leroy had selected a violent Day-Glo green, the hue of many a Halloween costume. On top of the neon he used shiny black paint to stencil a random but crowded pattern of three images: the bear from the California flag, the ubiquitous li'l lady on the doors of women's restrooms, and Riefenstahl's eagle symbolizing the Third Reich. I blinked when I saw the eagle. What were they teaching Leroy at school? It turned out that although he knew who Hitler was, he had never heard of Riefenstahl, and did not intend his eagle as a tribute to the *Jungsturm*. He thought that this fine eagle represented the world of skateboarding. As for the restroom woman, he just liked her. I accepted her into my life like Jesus.

Next Leroy liberally inscribed the walls with various Bible verses. Some, like Proverbs 3:5–6, I had memorized and treasured as a child: "Trust in the Lord with all thine heart; and lean not unto thine own understanding. In all thy ways acknowledge him, and he shall direct thy paths." But some of the verses begged closer scrutiny, perplexing as a rebus. I was mystified by I Kings 6:10, written on the wall above Leroy's bed: "And then he built chambers against all the house, five cubits high: and they rested on the house with timber of cedar." Or what about Exodus 15:9, printed on the ceiling? "The enemy said, I will pursue, I will overtake, I will divide the spoil; my lust shall be satisfied upon them; I will draw my sword, my hand shall destroy them." Frankly, I was a little concerned when I saw the lust and the destruction. And what did the Sword of the Destroyer have to do with the Woman of the Bathroom? Naturally I wanted to ask Leroy a series of pressing questions about his choices. But as the parvenu, I felt I couldn't cramp his style.

Then came the pièce de résistance. Into every available space between verse and eagle, sword and bear, Leroy scrawled a prepositional phrase that answered the tacit question, "Chloe Scholten, where do I love thee?" "In my crooked teeth." "With every step." "On my moped." "Between my toes."

Speech is a powerful thing, as Leroy must have surely experienced for himself when he reiterated his love for Chloe fifty times on the walls of his bedroom. Months after the breakup he came to me complaining that he still wasn't over Chloe. All around him his buddies were jumping to and fro from relationship to relationship, as lightly as frogs among lily pads. But here he was, eight months later, still not over his first love.

"I keep comparing other girls to her," he said mournfully.

"Well," I said, sensing my opportunity at last. "Have you taken care of all those declarations on the wall of your bedroom? Hard to reach closure when your own words still say that you'll love her forever."

In the intervening months Leroy's youth pastor, Zeke, had been teaching about the power of negative language. Zeke put it out there as a bold assertion of cause and effect: negative language prevents growth. Try and see if it is possible, he suggested, to feel gratitude when you're complaining. Let's say that your new stepson, calm as a Buddha, uses a clean linen napkin to sop up the leftover syrup on his plate. No matter how you slice it, that's irritating. But if I were to rehearse it, and keep telling it, and mention it every time I made *Rollkuchen*, the negative language would begin to puddle and stick. Two things would happen: I'd weaken my relationship with my stepson, and I'd sprout a vague, clinging self-pity, like a tiny pink mold in the grout of an otherwise clean shower. It's not that the people around us aren't irritating—they are, we are! It's that we shouldn't be *saying* so with our scary, mighty words. I suppose this is why complaining about someone always leaves me with a feeling of even greater injury, almost a toxic film of self-righteousness. I never feel better after a bitch session. In fact I always feel distinctly worse.

After Leroy heard Pastor Zeke teach on the power of negative words, I never heard him criticize his father or mother behind their backs. That's quite an achievement in a situation like Leroy's. When a kid shuttles back and forth between two families, you expect some gossipy complaint. I'd like to think that Leroy's restraint came from hard-won, prayerful practice. It is never easy to respect your elders in the daily dramas of life, especially when your buddies are complaining about their parents nonstop. Once I heard Leroy on the phone, telling a friend he was grounded. There was a pause. Surely here was a ripe moment to complain about Mitch's old-school parenting. But Leroy said only, "Yeah, man, it sucks. I'm grounded from Facebook until next week Saturday."

Now, months after the breakup, Leroy was ready to connect the dots. He astutely observed that fifty love declarations for a girl whose daddy had dumped him were unlikely to advance his social life or his self-esteem. So he got busy with primer and paintbrush.

I wish I could say that this episode had a happy ending. Alas, Leroy's prepositional yearnings, having been penned in indelible ink, rose up like mournful ghosts. The primer refused to cover the declarations of love. It seemed opaque enough at first. But when it dried, Chloe Scholten would persist, hazy but stubborn, coming back like Banquo. "Under my arm." "On my skin." "In my backpack." Leroy lost interest in this project after six coats of paint, but I began to take it personally. I even started shouting at young Ms. Scholten to cease and desist, as if she were some perverse and possessing spirit.

I did this in the style of a former assistant, Lily, who outed herself as a demon-exorcising, perfervid Christian when we were in Lithuania many years ago. Lily and I were stuck in a very small elevator in a Panevzys hotel. With us were five hotel employees who exuded a rich body odor, as if they had made a monthlong pact to forfeit underarm hygiene and any spice but cumin. "Cumin's okay! Tell Boris!" All were chain-smoking. One surly chap had a problem with Lily, who was biracial. I suspect slurs were made. Fortunately neither Lily nor I spoke Lithuanian.

Lily prayed out loud, in a fierce voice, for the stuck elevator. With passion and authority she commanded an evil spirit to come out of the cables. I had never heard anyone exorcise an elevator before. Neither had the other guys. They backed away a little. But Lily was just getting warmed up. She shouted that there was a Spirit of Limitation on the elevator, and she banished it by the authority vested in her by the risen Christ. I personally would have addressed the Spirit of Cumin before the Spirit of Limitation, but that was the difference between us. It had never occurred to me to blame the recalcitrance of everyday objects on powers and principalities, yet Lily would later detect Satan's malevolent hand in jammed copiers, flickering lightbulbs, and cupboards too high for her to reach. She exorcised everything from clogged toilets to leaky samovars. I'd like to think that Lily would have given me a Holy Roller hallelujah if she could have seen me in my stepson's bedroom wielding a paint roller and shouting, "Chloe Scholten, get thee behind me! Begone, palimpsest! I charge you, remove thy dinosaur naysaying ass to the La Brea Tar Pits!"

I stopped counting at twenty coats. However, I'm happy to report that today Chloe Scholten no longer haunts the walls of Leroy's old bedroom. When Leroy moved out, I used another gallon of primer beneath the new shade, a creamy neutral. It's the perfect color, soft and opaque, to accent the wall-to-wall shoe shelves that Mitch built me.

The stories we surround ourselves with can either move us forward or hold us back. A word in the mind is like a pebble in the shoe: both can bring our journey to a full stop. Leroy and I ended up learning a lesson about language. We both got stuck on words. I should never have asked if my friends from the dinner party believed in a literal fish. I should have asked what the story meant to them. Whoo boy. We can hold so tightly to language that our grip on it actually weakens communication. We can insist on our interpretation, but at what cost! How lovely it would be if we could hold our words loosely, like sand cupped underwater, carried away by the swift-moving current of meaning itself.

Like Leroy, we white out the past. We erase not our history, but its power to harm us. This is what it takes to move forward: an outpouring of grace, coat after coat, day after day, a willingness to keep going back to the room that speaks of our defeat. Faith is the hope that our work will have meaning, that someday our troubled rooms will be transformed.

TEN

The Poovey Voice

I'd been working hard on gratitude for some time, even before I started going back to church. In the months following my divorce, my best friend Lola emailed me every day from Italy. Lola was the sort of woman who was open to the concept of shamanic journeying and guided meditation, so she had plenty of reading suggestions for books that would promote wholeness, deepen my well-being, and embarrass me if someone I knew caught me reading them. ("My Friend Went on a Shamanic Journey and All I Got Was This Lousy T-Shirt!") Together Lola and I had read Eckhart Tolle, Wayne Dyer, Ted Kuntz, and Pema Chödrön. We had giggled through *The Secret*; we had visualized our chakras; and we had reorganized our homes according to the principles of feng shui. When Lola finally flew out to the States for our annual shopping spree the following summer, I was perfectly willing, in the name of holistic health, to consume raw peanuts and alfalfa tea, but Lola said you had to draw the line somewhere. So we passed on the alfalfa tea and kept on sipping whiskey sodas. They tasted just right with a nice homemade sour-cream chocolate cake. Abstemious we were not.

One of the first things we did was splurge on gratitude rings. We hadn't worn identical jewelry since we were eighteen, when we had both solemnly attached a miniature baby-blue clothespin to the arm of our sunglasses. This gesture proceeded from a late-night girlfest in which we made disclosures about frenzied kissing encounters with the theatrical Reggie Pointe. In college we all wanted to date Reggie Pointe because he was cocky as well as cute. Once when he was cast in *The Mikado*, he protested the cheesy bathrobes that the theater department tried to fob off as kimonos. Wrapped in his assigned navy bathrobe, Reggie appeared onstage, grinning like a goofus. He was holding a giant toothbrush and an outsize soap-on-a-rope. At eighteen we thought this the height of wit.

The baby-blue miniature clothespin was quick to catch on. It became a recognizable campus sign for a coed who had lived to talk about fooling around with Reggie Pointe. Word flashed from one dorm module to the next, and soon we were nodding in solidarity with our sisters whose sunglasses bore the telltale baby-blue clothespin. The tiny clothespins were pretty cute— they had a little diamanté action, see—and nobody actually regretted having fooled around with Reggie. But we pretended to groan at a hard life lesson: Reggie Pointe would stop at nothing! He would even come between *best friends*!

My dad told me that Reggie Pointe became a rich gentleman rancher who played hardball with the state legislature. The only other thing I heard about him was that at Reggie's brother's wedding, the bride had selected as a recessional the theme from

Star Wars. Naturally the inspirational coolness of Reggie Pointe had faded somewhat over time, vis-à-vis the state legislature and *Star Wars*, yet here we were, twenty-five years later, once again buying matching jewelry.

Lola and I wanted our gratitude rings to be beautiful, stylish, and inviting in texture. Every time we noticed or touched our rings we would stop for a moment and think, "I'm happy and grateful for my best friend!" For the duration of Lola's visit we commenced most sentences with "I'm happy and grateful—," as in "I'm happy and grateful that Reggie Pointe became a rich gentleman rancher who plays hardball with the state legislature, as opposed to an aging stand-up comic in LA." "I'm happy and grateful that I never slept with Reggie Pointe." ("You *didn't*?") "I'm happy and grateful that whenever Reggie Pointe's brother plays back his wedding video, he has to face the fact that he picked the theme song from *Star Wars*." And so on.

The gratitude rings consisted of nine silver freeform bars all in a tight picket line. The bars could spin round a horizontal axis, so the motion was perfect for counting off nine gratitudes. I counted and repeated like a rosary champion until one day several months later, in a department meeting at the college, all nine of my pretty silver bars snapped off the axis and splayed into my hand. "Oh no!" I exclaimed. "My gratitude ring! I'm so lucky it didn't break outside—I'd have lost the pieces!" My department chair pointed out that if the gratitude ring had given me that attitude, it was doing its job.

Lola and I kept up our spirits of thankfulness, but now, four years later, I figured I was ready to take on a more challenging form of gratitude.

I decided to put my money on the line. This required a mighty effort to quell logic and common sense. Everyone who tithes regularly says that when you give money to God, a miracle happens. Your 90 percent magically grows, like a sea monkey, and seems like much more than your 100 percent ever did. (That is, I cannot precisely quote anybody who has compared tithing to a sea monkey. But I feel an implied sea monkey. I feel a sea monkey *clinging* to this discussion, its skinny arms wrapped a trifle tight for comfort.)

I had never tithed. Occasionally I wrote a check, but always in the spirit of the classic mixed signal. I gave with one hand, and grasped with the other. For example, when Mitch and I first began dating, he came to me with a story about a teenage alto sax–player at his church. This young woman, Altagracia, had just returned from a mission trip to Honduras, where she had been so moved by the local church's music ministry that she had given away her one and only alto sax. Altagracia's family in the United States was not in a position to buy her a new instrument, and she, being fourteen, could not afford one herself. Altagracia was now unable to praise God with the worship team on Sunday mornings, said Mitch. What if he and I secretly bought her a new alto sax?

I said sure. Sure, of course. By all means! As long as I could make the check out to the church so that I could get a tax deduction.

Before I started tithing, that was my idea of giving. I had to make sure that even as I was giving, I was receiving—every jot and tittle that I could legally claim.

Contrast that story with this one. This next incident occurred two years later, after I had been tithing long enough for it to take root in my heart and mind. One Sunday morning working in the church nursery, I was rocking a little peanut in my lap. He snuggled like a cozy bunny and promptly fell asleep. He slept in my lap through the whole service. When his young mama came to collect him, she was yawning and sleepy, too. I said, "Sonia, now that Adan's had his nap, it's your turn."

Eyes strained and suddenly glassy, she said, "I wish!"

Turns out that she and her husband were sharing one single bed with their two-year-old, and nobody in her family was getting any quality sleep.

I don't know how old Sonia was when she got pregnant with Adan, but she looked about seventeen that day. Both she and Matias, her husband, had dropped out of high school to raise the baby. They had no family support. Matias worked full-time at Walmart. Sonia, pregnant again, couldn't work outside the home, as they couldn't afford childcare. When I asked Sonia what they needed most, she said it was a toss-up between a bigger bed for her and Matias, a separate bed for Adan, and a couch.

Mitch and I still had the queen bed and its brand-new linens from the guest suite in my old house, and also a spare single bed from my backup spare room. We had spare everything: sheets, duvet, pillows, mattress pads, bed frames, dressers, microwave, a TV, even Mitch's fake leather couch. "Let's hitch up the trailer," I said to Mitch after church, "and then we'll get Leroy to help us take a load of stuff over to their apartment."

Mitch and I were in complete agreement about giving this young couple as much as we could. And here's the kicker. At no time did I think of the tax deduction we could have taken if we had donated the furniture to Goodwill instead. In two short years of tithing, my position on charitable donations had stretched and grown. I had learned that giving with no strings attached can yield much more than a deduction ever could.

At the outset I wouldn't have imagined that one day I would be giving without thought of getting. My approach was motivated strictly by self-interest. Two thousand years of *lectio divina* had established that tithing increases gratitude. The daily practice of gratitude had already freed me from heavy things that were preventing my growth. By now gratitude had worked so well for me that I was willing to do almost anything to experience a greater degree of it. Because of the simple practice of counting gratitudes, I had been able to set down resentment, bitterness, and fear. Fantastic, right?

But I still had a vaguely neurotic desire to cling to the idea of My Money. Mennonites, of course, have a reputation for frugality. Doris Longacre's seminal cookbook *More with Less*, first published in 1980, has encouraged many of my tribe to embrace a greener, simpler lifestyle, nudging us back to our roots. (Hey, Mennonite eco-consciousness is accidentally hip!) From the Mennonites I learned money-saving skills such as sewing, gardening, canning, and cooking. I learned how to clip coupons, patch holes, and buy in bulk.

On the one hand, you can applaud this thriftiness as good stewardship. On the other, you can frown at frugality when it becomes both rigid and extreme. For example, I have a nipcheese uncle who refused to let his wife purchase a new dress for their fiftieth anniversary party. And I still remember the glorious day my parents finally broke down and took us to Disneyland. We were to return to the lockers at noon for a lunch of sun-warmed tuna sandwiches in a diaper bag. This part was Janzen business as usual. However, a special treat lay in store: my father solemnly gave us a quarter each. "You can spend this any way you choose," he said. This was in 1973, when a Coke cost twenty cents. My brother Aaron and I pooled our quarters to buy a single hot chocolate, which we split at a canopied table in the rain. Best hot chocolate I ever had.

As an adult I could make my own yogurt, whip up a batch of homemade window cleaner, and make really good broth from chicken bones. But I made up for it by spending all my mad money on art and Prada. Even in my new phase of spiritual growth, I was light-years from being able to ignore fashion. The usual position of enlightened seers and saints is to tell us seekers that fashion is a wicked consumerist trap to part the fool from her money. This from the Quaker author Richard Foster: "Hang the fashions! Buy what you need. Wear your clothes until they are worn out. Stop trying to impress people with your clothes and impress them with your life."

Much as I admire Richard Foster, he is assuming that there is only one reason to follow fashion. But what if you are drawn to beautiful clothes because you have an active aesthetic sense and because beauty makes you feel better about the world? And also, what if you had to wear dowdy underpants as a child, underpants that did not even comment on the days of the week? Eh, Dr. Foster?

So I was neither a nipcheese nor a profligate. What burdened me more than my actual financial obligations was the idea of money itself. I'd learned to live beneath my means, and I had paid off all my credit cards. But I still got tense around the subject of money. I held my checkbook tightly. I compulsively planned and budgeted and calculated. If I was saving for something, I'd find myself thinking about it during the day. When would I have enough? What could I give up to get the thing I wanted sooner? Which is all to say that my finances were exerting far too great an effect on my mind. Whether I was in my office or in my car, I'd often find myself prying my mind away from money, unsticking it like a kitten on a pant leg.

The thing we cling to is the thing that controls us. It was clear that I needed to detach.

In my listening and reading I heard over and over that tithing helps us detach. It demands a step of faith that jump-starts real spiritual growth. The universe rewards it. The spiritual benefits of tithing seemed the one issue that every church and theologian agreed on—and I'm not talking just about the big-haired crybaby televangelists with 18,000-square-foot McMansions (Hi, Mr. Copeland!). I'm talking about mature, scholarly theologians and church leaders whose lives have blazed gorgeous trails of service and altruism.

At church the pastor said, reasonably enough, that there were two ways to approach the subject of tithing. Either we could spin in circles, trying to get our minds around a principle that didn't make sense to those who had never tried it. Or we could become tithers and see for ourselves what all the fuss was about.

There's a singular verse in the Bible, the only one of its kind.

In it God makes a promise that invites us to test him. This verse is impossible not to read literally, because it is asking for a very literal thing from people of faith. It asks the people of God to bring a tithe, a word that literally means *one-tenth*. The implication is that the people should bring a tenth of all their resources—time and money and talent, whatever they've got—to the house of God.

The verse, Malachi 3:10, says, "'Bring the whole tithe into the storehouse, so that there may be food in My house, and test Me now in this,' says the Lord of hosts." But the Lord of hosts isn't finished yet. There's a nice surprise. God adds, "[See] if I will not open for you the windows of heaven, and pour out for you a blessing until it overflows." This verse stands alone because nowhere else in the Bible does God invite us to test him. People test God all the time, diddling around like Gideon with his damp fleece. However, this is the only time when *God* puts the invitation out there. This verse therefore anticipates our doubt, our skepticism, our clenched nervousness about money. It addresses these things directly. *Test me in this.* God knows how hard it is for us to let go of logic and sense. *Go on, test me.*

Some scholars point out that this commandment was directed only to those believers who were in a position to bring grain and food, farmers and the like. These scholars therefore conclude that this verse cannot apply to us today in modern faith communities. While I honor most methods of cultural criticism, I humbly suggest that these scholars have not tried tithing themselves. Once you have tried it—with vision and consistency and discipline—all arguments crumble like the proverbial walls of Jericho. Objection becomes a rubble of detritus to be swept away. Nobody who has tried cheerful, consistent giving would argue otherwise.

Logic would say, "O big shortsighted dummy! You cannot prosper if you keep giving your money away!" Just the other day I read a Suze Orman column in *O, The Oprah Magazine*. Suze Orman writes financial advice for the frazzled and overextended. A reader named Erin Mason had written in, wanting help with her family's unwieldy Frankenbudget. The Masons together were earning nearly $6,800 each month. Among their monthly expenditures Erin had listed a charitable donation of $86. Orman reported back that Erin Mason and her husband were not spending responsibly.

Orman specializes in making good solid sense. She advised a series of cuts, including the monthly charitable gift of $86. The Masons should curtail all unnecessary spending. Charitable donations were noble, but the Masons couldn't and shouldn't be making them on their budget.

Like the Masons, I couldn't afford to give money away. But the Bible made it sound as if we couldn't afford *not* to. *Test me in this! C'mon, you big baby! Bring it!* Knowing what I know now, I'd say that the Masons should have *upped* their charitable giving, not eliminated it altogether.

I want to be very clear on this point. I'm not saying that God withholds his blessing from people who don't tithe. We all know plenty of prosperous people—good people!—who do not give regularly to charity. Some experience tension surrounding their money; others don't. All I'm saying is: Here is the bizarre story of what happened to me.

༄

My decision wasn't attached to any epiphanic flash of insight. I just decided that I would take God at his word. I would test him. At worst I would lose 10 percent of one bimonthly paycheck, and come away with the same skepticism I already had. If I was going to step out in faith, and go to church, and, God forbid, eat Tater Tots at a potluck, then I might as well throw caution to the wind and see if the biblical message about tithing would hold up to the ins and outs of an economy in the pooper. Did a formal commitment to charitable giving *really* strengthen faith? The preacher said so.

But, then, preachers have a vested interest in getting congregants to tithe. Mennonites are suspicious of anything that smacks of prosperity theology. The essential message of prosperity theology—that God wants you to live a blessed, full life on earth as well as in heaven—is perfectly biblical, but I had always associated it with slick televangelists who flew around in $20 million private Cessna jets. Jesus, private jet; Jesus, private jet. The image didn't compute.

In 2007 Senator Chuck Grassley, on behalf of the US Senate Committee on Finance, formally requested statements of full financial disclosure from six of America's leading televangelists, all of whom preached the prosperity theology. The probe was designed to determine if these preachers were profiting personally from donations to their ministries. It was hard not to notice that some of the big-name preachers drove multiple Rolls-Royces, owned *two* private jets, and lived simultaneously in several multimillion-dollar homes. Moreover, the independent watchdog organization Ministry Watch gave several of the leading televangelists a grade of *F* for a lack of transparency. I love Ministry Watch. They're the *Consumer Reports* of Christian charities. Every year they investigate and grade more than five hundred ministries. I always check out their Donor Alert List (ministries on the scam) and their Shining Lights List (ministries with sterling records).

Cautious, I had already looked into the financial record of Mitch's church. It was solid. The church leaders weren't skimming fat salaries off the top. In fact I was impressed at their modest remuneration. The budget looked reasonable, even admirable. The church was involved in some wonderful programs that gave back to the community, and I loved the fact that it offered a food bank to families in crisis.

Still, to be safe I wrote my first check to an overseas service organization on the Shining Lights List at Ministry Watch. I photocopied the check for tax purposes and sat back to see if I would run out of grocery money approximately 90 percent into the month.

I didn't. Moreover, I hadn't done anything differently. Had I? The usual $100 had gone straight into savings. Mortgage, utilities, lawn guy, spider guy, two dinner parties. An irresistible leopard panty set on sale at Victoria's Secret. On what had I spent less? I studied my checkbook and couldn't see any areas of forfeiture. Perhaps it was a fluke. The next month I was expecting a whopping $269 association bill, so I would surely run out of cash without 10 percent of my net. When the first of the month rolled around, I was almost eager to write out another check to this same overseas ministry.

The next month right out of the gate I paid the association bill and all the other bills. Now a feeling of self-righteous expectation descended lightly as a mist. Anybody could see that *this* time, *this* month, I would come up short. I pointed this out to God helpfully. Meanwhile, the month was unfolding. Money was not materializing out of the nowhere into the here. Should I begin to cut corners? I decided not to. I would go on spending exactly as I had always spent. Malachi 3:10 made it sound as if I wouldn't have to scrimp. *I will open for you the windows of heaven, and pour out for you a blessing until it overflows.* There would be no enormous pot of cheap Cajun beans, not unless I could afford to stir in some yummy andouille sausage.

People always say that God is rarely early, but never late. With six days still to go until payday, I had $21.18 left in my checking account. Where was my blessing? I worried uneasily that maybe the blessing mentioned in Malachi 3:10 referred to a non-monetary blessing, perhaps more wisdom, more compassion, or a sudden noble calling to move to Tanzania. But I felt pretty sure that I did not want to ride around on a pikipiki with bugs smashed on my sunglasses.

Why sweat it? The worst that could happen was that I'd have to go six days on $21.18, which I had done plenty of times in grad school. There was food in the fridge, a tank full of gas. If Carla and Julie wanted to go out for lunch or drinks, we could always hang out on Julie's porch instead. Julie had a sociable porch. In this spirit I shrugged, changed into my karate pants, and went for a long walk.

I stopped by the mailbox on my way back in. There in the

mailbox lay a $400 check for a poetry publication. I had forgotten about it. Yay! But then: Hmmmm. Granted, a $400 check must always fall into the category called Blessing. But it wasn't as if this blessing had rained down out of a cold clear sky. I was *expecting* this check. Or anyway I would have been, if I hadn't forgotten it was coming.

Month after month I tithed and had enough. I couldn't predict how it would happen. It was always something different—refunds, credits, publications, invitations for public speaking. At about the eighth month I was ready to admit that Malachi 3:10 might represent a literal promise.

And I had begun to notice that something extra was happening. It was true that my remaining 90 percent always did seem like 100 percent. But more importantly, I was no longer worrying about money. Gone was the vague anxiety that I had always experienced whenever I opened my checkbook. In its place was a new feeling, airy and light as a lemon soufflé.

It was an amazing thing to be freed of financial worry, the inner frown, the calculator cramp. Four years ago, on the same visit when Lola and I had bought our gratitude rings, she and I reposed in the gathering dusk down on the lakeside platform at my then-home. When the sun was still high, we clambered down the steep stairs to the water's edge. We loaded ourselves down with pillows, bug spray, a self-help book, and a bottle of nice Shiraz. It was one of those perfect days when it's just you and your best girlfriend. The whole day had been charmed. In the morning we had worked out at my gym and then decimated a rotisserie chicken in the parking lot at Meijer. This is the kind of thing you do with only a very intimate girlfriend, especially if you have neither plates nor napkins. It helps to be so hungry that you hunch over the drumstick, chewing to the side, like a cat.

Down on the water platform we read aloud, freely interrupting each other to apply the self-help book to our own relationships. Eventually the fireflies flashed up from the shore, and it became too dark to read. We lapsed into dreamy silence, watching a flaming sun dip over the lake. A breeze stirred the chimes, and carp tails slapped the water. Suddenly, I don't know why, I began tugging at the wedding ring I had been wearing for fifteen years. My divorce had been finalized a few months earlier.

"You know what? I'm ready to take this off right now," I said.

"Then take it off," said Lola. "Let's have a toast." She poured the last of the Shiraz into our glasses.

"Wait." I stood up and walked to the platform's edge. Winding up like a pitcher, I lobbed my old wedding ring out over the water. It arced up in the shimmering dusk and fell, splashing down so far away that the *kerplunk* was barely audible.

"Done!" I said.

Lola offered catcalls and applause. "You just threw your wedding ring into the lake!"

"It's over." I turned back toward her, nodding, the nod gathering emphasis. "This means it's finally over!"

Lola caught the excitement in my voice and began singing a nonsense song to the tune of "Shake Those Simmons Down":

Ring in the lake, do-oh, do-oh!
Ring in the lake, do-oh, do-oh!
Let's feed the fish, do-oh, do-oh!
Shake that diamond down!

We twirled about, capering, a Lindy Hop of release and victory. I added my plain voice to her lovely one, improvising the lyrics. This was a Snoopy-dance, a victory dance. We cut a rug on that dock, in that tiny square of space. We shimmied and shook, snapped and spun, as if this dance had existed forever, and we already knew the steps.

Now, long after the throw-your-wedding-ring-in-the-lake dance, I remembered the feeling of sweet release and closure. I was in a different place, but the sensation was the same—it was a feeling of wholeness, a sense of God's perfect timing, a life chapter coming to a close. I intuited this even as I had known during chemo that I could live out the rest of my days without worrying about cancer. Strained finances would never furrow my brow again.

I wasn't expecting any more money than I usually earned. The amount of money in my bank account no longer seemed important, or even interesting. The shift wasn't in how much money I had. It was in how I felt about the money I did have. I finally understood worry as *irrelevant* to my actual finances. Had I ever been late with rent or mortgage? No. Had I ever gone hungry? No. Worry was *optional*. Altogether it seemed more effective to refuse worry.

When I was ready, God had whispered, "Go!" The timeliness made me marvel. It seemed to look back on all that had gone before, and to dismiss it gently, as when an auntie waves you a kind farewell down her driveway, even though you hardly ever visit. I had walked a long way in self-pity, always secretly blaming my money anxiety on the fact that I made so little as an academic. The truth was that my money anxiety had nothing to do with that. It was something that I had chosen to create and experience.

Steady giving changes your heart about money. It releases you from old patterns of tightfisted, myopic focus. Some folks think that it's enough to make one-time charitable donations now and then. But I wanted the whole enchilada, the feeling of joyful exhalation, and I knew I needed to make giving a habit. It is only when a new action becomes a habit that we invite change. It's as if the universe was waiting for me to stop being so controlling and petty about money. And then when I did release that pettiness, the money began to take care of itself. It came rolling in, just enough, at first. Then as I grew in spiritual fitness and in the beautiful habit of giving, it appeared in abundance.

When Mitch and I had been married half a year, my last book had been out for three months in hardback. Even if book sales were to earn the advance, which was unlikely for a newbie like me, I wouldn't receive royalties for another year. Every penny of the advance (except for the tithe) had gone to pay off my student loans.

On Saturday nights before church Mitch and I typically wrote out our tithing checks for the next morning, I in my study, Mitch in his. One night I got out a tithing envelope and began to write my check. But I stopped at the line on which you write the dollar amount. My fingers were itching. A voice sounded in my head, cheerful as Poovey when she shouts out some joyful and off-topic remark. My Poovey voice declared, "Let's tithe on the gross!"

Poovey is a large developmentally delayed woman in our Home Life group. Her caretaker is Lynette. I had received an excellent impression of both Lynette and Poovey. The first time I had met them, our Home Life pastor was leading a discussion about the notion of divine calling. We were gathered in Pastor Rick's living room on a Sunday evening. Suddenly Poovey leaned forward. Her weight rocked the recliner off its feet. She interrupted in a loud clear voice. "I have a praise!"

This church, as I have said, is not averse to interruptions. Pastor Rick courteously stopped what he was saying and encouraged Poovey to share her praise.

Poovey took a deep breath, summoning her focus. "I like my friends!" she announced. "My friends are good friends! The Lord has blessed me with some good friends!"

"Well, praise the Lord for good friends," Pastor Rick said.

A consensus of nods and assents around the group: yes, yes, we all praised God for good friends. Friends were good. So good. Lynette reached over and patted Poovey on the arm. This was when I decided I really liked them both.

A couple of weeks later at the church picnic, Lynette asked me for my recipe for corn pudding. I loved this freedom about church potlucks. At non-catered artsy functions it was impolite to ask for a recipe. You could admire, and chew thoughtfully, and remark on the happy combination of balsamic reduction and fresh watermelon, but you would never ask anybody for an actual recipe. Not so at church potlucks. Of course, there were the occasional landmines to sidestep: canned-green-bean casseroles with onion crispees, or the marshmallow fruit "pizza." But even among the ladies who wore matching capris and tank tops, those days were mostly over. I was having fun adapting favorites for potluck fare—a roast veggie medley here, a faro salad there.

Lynette and I had been chatting about corn pudding for about three minutes when, wham, she suddenly revealed that she suffered from chronic constipation. My mother might make such a disclosure on very short acquaintance. However, in my social world people do not discuss functions of the bowel, especially with people they barely know. My friends would be more likely to risk a controversial remark about politics than a remark about their lower intestine. I wasn't sure what to do, what to say—what would Jesus do? "Do unto your intestine as you would have it do unto you."

I had been eating what Marilynne Robinson would call the Presbyterian Three-Bean Salad, but now I put down my spoon. Swallowing hard, I said, "Exercise is supposed to help with that. What do you do for exercise, Lynette?"

She would have no subject change. She waved her hand, as if to dismiss exercise and all its putative advantages. "Laxatives are so hard on your gut! Prunes help when I get constipated, but you can only eat so many."

This reminded me of a time when, living with a girlfriend in France, I had determined that you can eat seven big prunes a day without undue intestinal turbulence. More than seven—say, twenty-seven—and you'd be in for a bumpy ride in the land of pay toilets and single-square toilet paper. If I could bring myself to discuss the Holy Spirit in public, could I not also bring myself to address the occasional interlude of bilious indigestion? I went for it. I told Lynette my prune story.

"—and we were so fatigued from that awful train ride that we lay down on the grass outside the station and fell asleep."

"I DON'T CARE FOR PRUNES," Poovey declared, as if she had been offered some. "PRUNES ARE NOT DELICIOUS. I AM READY TO GO HOME NOW." She was using her outdoor voice, although her hands were folded quietly in her lap. Lynette patted Poovey's arm again and rose to gather the plastic cutlery and spicy guacamole. I came away from that picnic thinking I had had a very nice time indeed.

Poovey voice or no, I had no intention of tithing on the gross. Such an increase would involve giving two hundred dollars more than my regular tithing check. Mitch and I needed all of my salary, minus the net tithe, for monthly expenses. I was sure of this. Yet I got up and briskly walked over to my files, as if I had meant to do this all along. Here was a paycheck stub. I calculated the tithe on the gross, completed my check, and sealed the little envelope. Where would we get this extra two hundred dollars? My Poovey voice fired up again. "Hi there, God! You're my friend!"

Then I went into Mitch's office to break the news that I had just made a weird financial decision without consulting him. "Guess what I just did."

"Made your Aunt Mag's chewy cashew squares?"

"No. I just tithed on the gross, and I'm not sure why."

"Honey, *I* felt led to tithe on the gross tonight." He did not seem surprised that we had both been propelled to this act on the same Saturday evening, within minutes of each other, and without having discussed it. "God is stretchin us, callin us to step up on our givin." He paused, doing math in his head. "It might be kinda tight this month."

One of Mitch's and my daily prayers is for like-mindedness and unity as a couple. Here was like-mindedness! We were both impressed with the Spirit's subtlety, though I spent some serious time wondering why the Spirit would enter my conscious mind in the voice of a large developmentally delayed woman. Surely the Poovey voice was a projection from the deep mind, the one that didn't want to believe that spiritual revelations were so sublimely simple. God should have the deep polished voice of James Earl Jones. Everybody said so. And by "everybody," I mean "Carla and me."

I've always been attracted to the developmentally delayed as a group. Their cheer, their clarity, and their specifically articulated desires underscore the fact that our natural state is joy, and that humans are capable of clearly asserting their wants and needs. It's taken me a long time to controvert gendered Mennonite patterns of passive-aggressive communication. In fact I'm still working on that. My developmentally delayed cousin Bernie, now in his late forties, always makes me smile. What a lovely outlook he has, even though there's a hole in his heart and his health is poor!

When I was trying to explain the Poovey voice to my mom over the phone, I compared Poovey's peaceful élan to my cousin Bernie's. "I love the clarity that developmentally delayed folks have!"

"Bernie's not developmentally delayed," said my mother.

"What do you mean?" I asked blankly.

"He's not delayed. There's no retardation there. Bernie just has problems with his health."

"Mom, Bernie's developmental delay is *unmistakable*! Don't you remember how at Aunt Trude's wedding he ran tight circles around the pop-up trailer, shouting 'MANURE, MANURE'? He did that for, like, an *hour*."

"He was excited. That's a perfectly normal thing for a little boy to do."

"But he ran all goofy in the cousin relays!"

"He just wasn't very coordinated," my mother explained. "Being a bad athlete doesn't make you mentally retarded! If he were retarded, he would need a caretaker, and he'd have to live in a home. But Bernie's been living on his own for years."

"Oh!"

"He can't work full-time because of his health, but he has a part-time job as a crossing guard."

Apparently I had been under a forty-year misapprehension about my cousin Bernie. I wondered if I ought to beg his pardon. At our infrequent family reunions I had always been very, very careful to pitch conversational softballs. With sudden shame I recalled those times when I had waved excitedly at Bernie, patting the picnic bench, hoping he would come sit beside me. Bernie was probably thinking, "Geez, Cousin Rhoda sure ain't the sharpest knife in the drawer!"

Now that I knew Bernie wasn't developmentally delayed, I liked him even more. Imagine the chops it takes to live from a place of simplicity when the mind longs for complexity! I'd lay odds that even with a crappy crossing-guard job, Bernie would tithe with joy.

The Mennonite church in which I had been raised never taught that the blessing is literal—that is, financial. In my childhood church the main benefits of tithing had been framed as the twin perks of spiritual growth and character-building discipline. However, I was now teetering on the brink of a freaky cause-and-effect supposition. To wit, if you tithe steadily, your money problems will vanish. I thought about rephrasing. If you tithe steadily, your money problems will *seem* to vanish.

In passing I had heard a couple of Mennonite theologians dismiss this equation as a watered-down, avaricious, Americanized version of the gospel, the blab-it-and-grab spiel of shysters hoping to fleece a money-motivated culture. "Send us your gift of twenty dollars and God will honor you with much more! Plus we'll say a nice prayer over your check. And, hey! We've got some great bayou swampland to sell! Start your own crawdad business!"

However, by now I had a couple of years' inductive evidence to suggest that the literal interpretation was valid. It made no sense whatsoever. The literality continued to apply as we tithed on the gross month after month. Yet this time there were no miraculous checks, no paid public-speaking opportunities. Tithing on the gross called for real, non-negotiable cutbacks. Good-bye fancy salmon dishes, hello homemade Indian entrees strong on chickpeas and spinach! See ya Aveda, howdy no-name shampoo that smelled a little like a diaper! No longer did I shop for exceptionally long pants. (I'm very tall.) Mitch stopped buying hunting equipment altogether. When Leroy's backpack broke, we told him that a punk rockabilly safety-pin look was kind of fresh.

Curiously calm about all this forfeiture, I made a new rule for myself: no new clothing, period. If I couldn't find it at a consignment store, I'd pass. This was my biggest financial challenge yet, as I am a serious shopper, with a long history of unwise and frivolous purchases. But what can you say when in an odorous thrift store you put your hand out and a gorgeous MaxMara skirt jumps into it? A MaxMara skirt, perfectly current and in excellent shape, in my size, for seven dollars? I interpreted the MaxMara skirt as a big fat thank-you from the universe: "Dear Rhoda, thanks for giving! Now let me give you something!"

We had enough every month, even when the numbers shouldn't have added up. But we did have to give stuff up in order to tithe on the gross. It was as if God had made tithing easy at first, and then had upped the ante as we grew in the spirit of giving. At first we gave with a what-the-hell attitude, as when you are getting ready to skydive for the first time. Here goes nothing! But after a while we began to give with an inexplicable joy, the same kind of joy that a besotted woman feels when she is presenting her new husband with a sandwich on a little tray. "God, I got something tasty for you! Hope you like it!"

In a couple of months we got used to the bigger tithe. Then it felt as if we had always lived like this, eager to give as much as we could. The increased giving soon seemed a mild inconvenience in comparison to the rich peace we felt when dropping those checks in the offering. Had my wardrobe suffered? No, it had improved! I even began to adjust to the diaper shampoo. In a certain shower moment, with your eyes closed and your hair lathered, it smelled not unlike a steamed dumpling.

One Sunday at church Elder Justine outlined a new fundraising project that would allow the church to pay off its mortgage entirely, so that more could be given to overseas missions and the local food bank. Instead of soliciting checks on the spot, Elder Justine asked the congregation to go home and pray. She said this money was not to come out of strained budgets and daily living expenses. Rather, it was to come from the surprising and miraculous providence of God. Then she invited folks to come up to the front of the church to take a gift envelope. Each envelope, in a perfect world, would represent a unit of five hundred dollars. Mitch went forward. I knew even before he reached the front that he would come back with two envelopes.

We didn't have an extra thousand dollars. What we did have, though, was faith in the surprising and miraculous providence of God. In the past whenever I had questioned the efficacy of prayer, Mitch had quoted James 5:16: *The prayer of a righteous man availeth much*. I would never call myself righteous, but it was true that I was trying. I was on the path. The work of practicing gratitude had freed me from petty grudge holding. I had forgiven old hurts, and I had sought to make amends for hurting others dear to me. I knew that people of faith can't expect to be blessed if they are still hanging on to resentments the size of Texas. But I had left Texas. I was in a different state now, a weird one, where I'd actually rather have cancer than a grudge.

"That thousand bucks'll show up here in a minute, honey," said Mitch. "If God wants us to drop a thousand-dollar check into the offering, he'll give us an extra thousand somehow."

The next Sunday morning during the service Sister Shekinah stood and made a gesture that I love: an imperious summoning of the microphone, hand high and visible as a semaphore. Sometimes she presented a deep-voiced declaration from the Almighty. The Pentecostals called this "bringing a word from the Lord." When Sister Shekinah rose to speak in the middle of the service, resplendent in a ruby sequined beret, everybody leaned forward on the edge of their seats.

"There is breakthrough a-comin'!" she shouted into the mike. "The Holy Spirit says BREAKTHROUGH is yours if you'll claim it! The Holy Spirit says the time is now to ask! Just ask and you'll receive! BREAKTHROUGH is here, BREAK-THROUGH is now, BREAKTHROUGH is yours!"

People were singing and swaying to begin with, but when Sister Shekinah uttered this message, the worshippers stomped and clapped and danced. They often paused to applaud the Lord—"Let's give God a big clap!"—but their response now was astonishing, even in a house that celebrated its freedom to shake booty for the glory of God. Those who had remained in their seats now rose and surged forward to cluster around the altar. A couple of kids began sprinting back and forth across the front of the church, elbows pumping, a frenetic energy rising. One of the elders, a mature man of fifty, joined them, chuffing full-tilt back and forth across the sanctuary.

As strange as this was, Mitch and I promptly bowed our heads and prayed for breakthrough. We claimed it. We owned it. I raised my own arm as if beckoning to a busy server. "Here! Over here! I need a fork!" We went home smiling and expectant.

Three days later I got a miraculous phone call from my editor. My book, published six months ago, had made the *New York Times* bestseller list.

How was this even possible? I hadn't written about vampires

falling in love, or vampires biting sexy but unsuspecting admirers! At no time had I even alluded to vampires, their hopes, their dreams, their netherworldly longings! I was an academic with a narrow readership—mostly gentlemen eggheads who had checked me out online and who used words like *lacustrine* and *plebiscite*. What's the opposite of a vampire? I'll tell you! A sentence diagram! I published essays about *grammar*, for God's sake!

My book jumped to #1. It stayed on the bestseller list for almost a year. You may be sure that we dropped the first thousand dollars into Elder Justine's envelopes, shaking our heads in astonishment.

Could I explain our recent prosperity in another way? Sure. I could point to the fact that I was surrounded and supported by seriously competent professionals. I had the best editor and agent of all time. I could attribute the success of that book to their savvy guidance. Or I could say that this success came about as the result of years of craft and study.

And yet. And yet. Many authors like and respect their editors and agents, and heed their voice. What author hasn't applied their hints? What author has neglected to hone her craft? All authors hone their craft. Except maybe the vampire authors. Hopefully those vampire books do not result from years of rigorous training. I'd like to think they were written in Cozumel, when the author was enjoying a powerful margarita.

When my editor called me, I was serving as poet-in-residence at a small distant college. The college was hosting me in a lakeside cabin, tiny and plain. The cabin had been built in the 1930s, and I loved its split-log modesty. Three hooks on the bedroom wall substituted for a closet, so I was wearing pretty much the same thing every day to teach. The wee kitchen invited the plainest fare—yogurt and fruit, dates and peanut butter. For three weeks my life pared down to essentials. All I did was read, teach, eat, and sleep. Sometimes I graded papers in a plastic chair by the water's edge. Sometimes I graded them in a plastic chair by a firepit. Sometimes I graded them in bed, wearing both my sweaters at the same time. It was therefore hard to get my mind around what my editor was telling me: Bestseller. Abundance. Options. All for one who at that very moment was dipping a date directly into a jar of peanut butter.

Mitch picked up even though he usually lets all work calls go to voice mail. I shouted without preamble into his ear, "We made the list! We're a *New York Times* bestseller! Do you know what this means? We can afford to fix the icemaker!"

"I'm gettin a new ink cartridge!"

"I'm dumping the diaper shampoo!"

"We can give more than a thousand bucks!"

Both of us felt it then. Something had changed, and it wasn't the money. Breakthrough.

ELEVEN

⚮

Whippersnapper

At the beginning of our relationship it was hard for me to get my mind around Mitch's built-in drive to kill. Having been raised among pacifist Mennonites, I couldn't quite grasp the reality of Mitch's inner predator. Once when we were driving around town together doing errands, we passed the local Travel Lodge Motel. Driving by this establishment makes me throw up my hands in disgust, New Yorker style. I used to swear, but now I make the universal gesture of urban loathing. The reason is that the outside facade of the Travel Lodge has been decorated with many fake wooden bear cubs. The cub décor is intended to seem woodsy and winning, as with a bear jamboree. The cubs dandle from the windows and clamber on the balconies as if to say, cutely, "Let us in, we are bear cubs!"

Mitch looked at me inquiringly when I made The Gesture.

"Show me a marketing director who thinks fake wooden bear cubs are adorable, and I'll show you a woman who scrapbooks with glitter and bees," I said. "Every time I drive by this place I question why a benevolent God could let bear cubs happen to an innocent building."

"I like 'em."

"Pardon me?"

"I like them bears all right."

"But they're the worst representation of kitsch this side of Medieval Times!"

"Be nice to stick 'em at forty yards," he mused.

"You want to *shoot* them? With a bow and arrow?"

"Good target practice," he said.

When Mitch was hunting, a glorious primal surge took over his mind and body. He said that the instinct came down on him as a powerful stealth. His pulse roared and his chest hammered. Instinctively he stalked and focused, tracked and shot. What's a gal to do when her husband proudly brings her an actual bear in a Hefty bag? Four Hefty bags, to be precise? Being Mennonite, I know my way around most cuts of meat, and in theory a quartered bear in a Hefty bag should not faze me. But it's a little weird. If anybody's interested, I now have recipes for bear burgers, bear steak, and bear lasagna. I'm feeling my way gingerly.

It would be hypocritical for me to object to hunting, as I eat meat. But I can't even imagine being hardwired to kill. Mitch says he has to hunt the same way that I have to write; it's a blind force that propels and fuses him to the bow. Whenever I think of my own fierce compulsion to sit down at my desk, I whisper Dylan Thomas's famous line, changing the last word: "The force that through the green fuse drives the flower / Drives my green page." I of all people should understand the idea of a cosmic compulsion. Yet the interest in the death of living entities seems fundamentally foreign to me, and cruel. The invisible code of profiting from such death becomes visible when Mitch calls attention to the killing and the dying. When the cat drags in dead rodents, Mitch compliments the cat. "Lars! Good boy, bit his head right off!"

Once Lars came up the stairs yowling the victory yowl. How he managed a throaty war cry with a live chipmunk in his mouth I do not know, but he deposited this stunned chipmunk at Mitch's feet. Mitch was at that moment arriving home from work, coming through the front door in his heavy work boots. Always cool in an emergency, he cast aside his lunchbox and flung his sweatshirt over the chipmunk. He promptly lifted his boot and tramped on the chipmunk's head.

Thankfully I was not home to witness this. I was appalled when told about it.

"You stepped on its *head*?"

He nodded. "It was gonna die anyway. I had to act fast, or it would have gone tearin through the house. Them critters are hard to catch."

I can see stepping on a spider. But a chipmunk? "Jesus would not have stepped on a chipmunk's head," I asserted.

"I disagree."

"You're telling me Jesus *would* have stepped on a chipmunk's head?"

"I think so. If he had a good reason. Maybe if Lars had brought it inside the temple. Jesus meant business when he was clearin out the temple with the whip. Jesus could put it on a chipmunk."

Here was the Jesus whip again! We had often gone over our

differing views on nonviolence. I'd always believed in a Christological model of nonviolent problem solving. But whenever I brought up the biblical pacificism of Jesus, Mitch was quick on the draw with John 2:13–16, in which Jesus clears out the temple money changers with a whip. Jesus is all worked up because a bunch of merchants have turned God's house into a marketplace, and he angrily drives them all out.

Who am I to say that Jesus would not have driven out a whole crowd of unholy chipmunks, snapping his whip in righteous fervor? Growing up, I never heard a single sermon preached on the Jesus whip. Without ministerial guidance I had imagined Jesus pitching a harmless hissy fit in the middle of the temple, cracking his whip for cranky emphasis. In my imagination Jesus wasn't actually *hurting* anybody. When I explained this vision to Mitch, he laughed at me. "Jesus *drove* those money changers out of the temple," he said. "Honey, when you drive someone, you don't just wave a whip around. You *use* it."

The various versions of this verse have historically been used to justify violence, military action, and even vigilante justice. But I didn't see how Whippersnapper Jesus gave us the right to take the law into our own hands.

"Why wouldn't Jesus command the unruly chipmunks to cease and desist, as he did the winds and the waves?"

"Because he's mad at the chipmunks."

An excellent feature in a husband is his willingness to discuss hypothetical scenarios involving Jesus.

"I think Jesus should be mad at Lars for having brought the chipmunks into the temple in the first place. Or maybe he should be mad at whoever installed the cat door in the temple."

"You don't think Jesus would have shot the raccoon?"

A raccoon had been sneaking in our cat door, eating freely from the buffet I provided for the cats. Their downtick in hygiene had been commanding—crumb trails, footprints, dirty water—but I had thought the cats were just going through a phase, like Leroy. Mitch, a true woodsman, could tell at a glance that this was no phase. He said, "That ain't no downtick. That's a coon."

When we went to bed, he left the light on, his bow propped against the door. At 5:10 a.m. he stiffened. Our bedroom was upstairs, a whole house away, but he whispered, "I just heard the cat door." Off he went to stalk the intruder. He arrowed the raccoon there inside the house. Shot clean through, the raccoon pooped a little, then expired in the yard. My husband and I clearly disagreed about raccoon management.

"When you have a coon sneakin in and eatin your cat food, you need to man up. Jesus would not have let that critter eat all his wife's cat food."

"How do you know that the cat belonged to Jesus' wife, and not to Jesus? Personally, I think Jesus was comfortable enough with his masculinity to own a cat."

"Nah, honey. Jesus would have a dog."

I loved discussions like this.

"What kind of a dog?"

"A shepherd," he said seriously, as if there could be no other contenders.

"Jesus entered his shepherd in a dog show," I said tentatively. "Jesus tied a smart red hanky around his dog's neck."

"Nah. None of that."

I tried again. "Jesus carried a plastic bag when he walked his shepherd."

Mitch was willing to consider this. It was one of the reasons I loved him.

Once when Lola came to visit from Italy, Mitch took me and her out to a backwoods range, to teach us how to shoot. Like me, Lola had been raised Mennonite, but she now lived with her Italian artist husband in an apartment in a seventeenth-century Bolognese villa. She sang opera—not the kind that Mitch and I freely improvised, but real opera, with years and years of language, travel, and training. If I was wearing a perfect embroidered *salwar kameez* from Mumbai, or a vivid tasseled sheath from Namibia, it was because Lola had procured them for me on her many travels.

You'd think that with all this cosmopolitan gloss, Lola would no longer manifest behaviors that were visibly Mennonite. However, I find plenty of evidence to suggest that though you may take the girl out of the Mennonites, you can't take the Mennonite out of the girl. We can run, but we can't hide. Beneath Lola's stylish surface, she was still subject to many of the same values, anxieties, and family protocols that had shaped her childhood and mine. To wit, Mennonites don't shoot. We don't even *think* about shooting.

Mitch understood that my friend and I had been raised as pacificists, and he knew that I was antiwar. But he saw this Mennonite tenet as a circumstance of privation, like growing up without rock-n-roll or Hostess Ding Dongs. He was thinking that it was a darn shame we'd never been given the opportunity to hold and shoot a gun. It would be liberating for us! Once he had mentioned that the Bullet Hole was offering concealed-weapon classes for women, as if he secretly hoped I might be the sort of wife to carry a small revolver in my purse along with emergency dental floss.

Lola and I were not thinking about liberation as Mitch set us up with protective headphones and walked the target out fifty yards. In a spirit of tentative goodwill she and I had agreed to come, but now we exchanged nervous glances beneath our plastic safety goggles. We had been taught that guns existed for one thing and one thing only: death. At that moment Lola was shouldering a magnum twelve-gauge pump shotgun with a three-inch shell. Beside her I had both hands wrapped around the grip of the second-largest handgun on the market, a .44-caliber Ruger Super Red Hawk, whose rounds Mitch had thoughtfully made himself on a home reloading press in the basement.

My husband was calm, safe, and highly trained. Lola and I were not scared that we would misfire. We were scared that we would fire.

At this point I would like to insert a family story that illustrates the long complicated history Mennonites have on the subject of violence and nonresistance. What I am going to tell you is a true story. I first heard it from a Mennonite historian un-related to me. Some months later a cousin who knew I was interested in genealogy sent me a primary text of the same account. At the behest of the man telling the story—my elderly uncle, now deceased—my cousin had prepared a verbatim transcript. This elderly uncle was the second son of my grandfather Jacob Janzen, and, although very young, my uncle was present when the incident happened. There were many witnesses.

Jacob Janzen's family had been living in a prosperous agricultural Mennonite settlement in Ukraine since the late eighteenth century. They had relocated to Ukraine from Prussia because Catherine the Great had promised them religious freedom. It was a good bargain for everybody: the Russian tsarina would strengthen her southern border with tidy agricultural settlements, and the Mennonites would finally be able to practice their faith in peace.

The central tenet of this faith was nonviolence. Mennonites refused to fight. This position did not arise out of cowardice or an unpatriotic spirit. It arose out of the deeply held conviction that Jesus modeled a different kind of life, one that would turn the other cheek, even to martyrdom. When civil authorities came after Mennonites with beheadings and burnings, the Mennonites were forced to articulate a corporate response to violence. Would they fight back? With remarkable unity they decided they would not. Not now. Not ever. They would go to the stake singing.

So for centuries pacifism had been not just a way of life, but the organizing principle by which Mennonites had lived. And for over a hundred years in imperialist Russia, all was well. Well, that is, for the Mennonites. What's not to love about a lifestyle so prosperous that it allows you to feel superior to native peasants who don't even clean their yards?

However, this Mennonite complacency deflated sharply during the Bolshevik Revolution of 1917. Lenin's Red Army collided with the White Army, who were loyalists to the tsar. In the ensuing chaos up sprang an epic maverick named Nestor Makhno, who managed to raise his own army. He was like a brutal Robin Hood, dedicated to empowering the poor by murdering, raping, and plundering the rich. In this equation he and his men were the deserving poor and the Mennonite farmers were the despicable rich. I should point out that, comparatively, the Mennonite farmers *were* rich. Much has been written on the figure of Nestor Makhno, so I'll sum up his violent incursions by saying that his style was to sweep into an unsuspecting Mennonite village, order a pregnant woman tied to the back of a wagon, and drag her to her death while the woman's husband and children were forced to watch. In one of the attacks there was only one survivor in the entire village, a baby.

In the face of these atrocities some of the outraged Mennonite men organized a *Selbstschutz*, a self-defense unit that was hotly contested by those who would rather die in Christ than live under the curse of violence. To the young whippersnappers of the *Selbstschutz*, the old guard said, "You might be able to save the village from violence one night. But what happens when Makhno's men interpret your defense as an out-and-out declaration of war? They'll be back, and next time these four hundred will be four thousand. Don't answer violence with violence! Don't offend the Lord by sinking to the level of these monsters!"

The hot young men persisted, as young men will. They had some guns, a few horses, no grenades. They mounted a watch in every Mennonite village. One night in 1920, at the height of the political chaos, the watchman sounded the alarm in my grandfather's village. In swept the Makhovschina on horseback, hungry, teeming with lice and typhoid. They weren't expecting an armed defense. They were thinking of food, pretty wives and daughters, the pleasures of sticking it to The Man.

From strategic hiding places the *Selbstschutz* opened fire. Makhno's men were falling left and right, not knowing where the shots were coming from. The young men whooped in triumph when the remaining bandits wheeled their horses to beat a hasty retreat. When the villagers finally understood that the danger had passed, they surged into the square. Among them was my grandfather's first wife, Martha Schmidt Janzen. Already the men were arguing about what to do with a wounded bandit, shot but not dead. This one lay bleeding on the ground. A Mennonite man, the father of three girls, was holding a pistol to the bandit's head, execution-style, shouting, "He came to kill and rape! If we let him live, he'll come back and finish the job!"

Several of the old guard, sick with grief, covered their eyes rather than see one of their own commit murder in cold blood. Then my grandfather's wife stepped forward. "Bring him to our house," said Martha. "We can decide what to do with him later. I'll look after him." The leaders looked around. Where was Jacob, Martha's husband? He wasn't present to speak for her. But something in her voice, a quiet conviction, persuaded them to lift the bandit into a wagon for transport to the Janzen home.

Martha was not a native Ukrainian Mennonite. She was a German who had studied nursing in Berlin. For the past nine years she had been housemother at a Ukrainian Mennonite hospital, and when she said that she would take care of the wounded bandit, the Mennonites knew she could. But they shook their heads, whispering at such a decision when she had three young children in the house. The villagers were glad to ride away from the louse-ridden man, relieved of an agonizing life-and-death decision.

All through that long winter Martha nursed the bandit, whose condition was critical. She spoke no Russian, and he no German, but they managed to communicate. My grandfather, Jacob, Martha's husband, did speak Russian. Once at Martha's urging he sat down and translated to his captive audience those passages from the New Testament that have to do with peacemaking. The bandit understood enough to know why he had been spared.

In spring, when he was well enough to leave, the bandit kissed Martha's cheek in farewell, telling her that he would always be grateful to the "Little Mother."

For three more war-torn years Martha picked lice, boiled sheets, and did what she could to ease suffering in a village decimated by famine and privation. In 1923 she contracted typhus herself and passed swiftly for one who had been impervious to death and disease for so long. Although in 1923 there were funerals every day—sometimes bodies stacked and abandoned in the street—the villagers showed up en masse for the funeral of this good woman whose silent witness had saved so many.

In the middle of Martha's funeral, just as her hastily assembled pine coffin was being lowered into the earth, the alarm sounded. Those with guns swiftly prepared. But on the horizon only one Makhnovite appeared. They saw a lone man on horse-back riding hell-for-leather toward the village. The mourners thought he was a lunatic as he plunged onto the main thor-oughfare without slowing his pace. He rode *ventre à terre* to where they stood gathered at the cemetery and reined his horse so abruptly that he fell forward. Without acknowledging any of the Mennonites present, he fell to his knees at the grave, lifting his voice in loud lament, according to Russian custom. "Lit-tle Mother, Little Mother!" the man wept, crying and rocking. The villagers knew then who this bandit was, and although none raised their voices in lament like his, many understood the pro-found nature of his grief. And they were grieving too—not just for Martha, but for a precious value that had gone the way of violence and retribution.

Into the stillness Lola shot the rifle, hitting the paper but not the target, grabbing her shoulder at the emphatic recoil. She glanced over and shook her head slightly. "That's enough for me," she said brightly to Mitch. "Now I can say I've shot a gun."

Mitch looked at me expectantly. I tried, I really did. I sighted the target, I steadied my hand. But I couldn't bring myself to squeeze the trigger.

"Don't be scared, honey," Mitch encouraged. "Just move with the recoil. It won't hurt you."

But I could think of no one whom it would hurt more.

∽

This story, like all stories, has an inconclusive ending. One evening two years into my marriage Hannah called to tell us that the night before they'd had a prowler. *Prowler* wasn't really the word for it, as there was very little prowling involved. It was a surprising incident for Hannah and Phil's affluent, quiet neighborhood. Their neighbors discussed it for days afterward.

At about 2:00 a.m. the dog suddenly went ballistic. I hope my sister will forgive me for saying that her dog, Dexter, is cripplingly stupid. He has a long history of moves no self-respecting canine would make. However, throughout the stupidest moves, such as finding and eating rat poison, or running full tilt into traffic, he usually maintains a dignified silence. On this night he began barking and lunging at the big bay window downstairs in the great room. Hannah and Phil rose at once and went downstairs to see what was wrong.

On their patio in twelve-degree weather, snow all around, stood a barefoot man engaged in a heated discussion with a trim line of arborvitae. The man seemed to think the shrubs were arguing with him, but it was hard to tell because he was speaking a language they couldn't place. Although he was wearing only a thin T-shirt and jeans, he did not appear to be cold.

Phil peered out the glass. "There's a barefoot guy on the patio. Looks like he's talking to the arborvitae."

"Ask him what he wants."

Phil cracked the door and said, "Dude, what's going on?"

The man turned and smiled warmly, switching to a fluent, barely accented English. "I have a job," he said. "It's a pretty good job, for a job."

"Time to go home," said Phil firmly. "Why don't you leave before I call the police?"

The man regarded this as an invitation. Phil quickly shut and dead-bolted the door, but the prowler came right up to the glass and began rattling the knobs. "I come here all the time," he explained to Phil through the French doors.

Hannah called the police. While they waited for the officers to arrive, they put on their fuzzy robes and made tea. They turned on all the outside lights. Meanwhile the employed prowler tried each and every window on the ground floor, reverting to his native language but occasionally offering some generic advice in English such as, "Match the grout to the tile, or you'll be sorry!" and "No looking back if you got lumps!"

Hannah doesn't know if the officers arrested him or just took him home. He was a local contractor with a substance abuse problem, and they never heard any more about the matter. Hannah concluded the story by saying, "I'm just so glad Allie slept through it! Imagine being fourteen and waking up to a guy rattling the doors!"

Hannah's story was on my mind, but lightly so, because I too lived in a safe neighborhood. One night Mitch and I went to bed after listening to a Great Courses lecture. We were big fans of the Great Courses. Taught by distinguished university professors, each series consisted of thirty or so half-hour lectures, perfect food for thought before bed. Mitch and I took turns choosing the topics. When it was my turn, they were always about the bubonic plague, medieval hygiene, or Renaissance marriage law. When it was Mitch's turn, they were always about hoplite phalanxes, battering rams, or the Crusades.

That night we were listening to Dr. Gary Fagan on my laptop. The lecture was entitled "The Assyrian War Machine," from a course called *Great Battles of the Ancient World*. It was the seventh lecture of the series, and perhaps the third warrior course we'd seen, so by now I was used to it all—you name it, heads on a stick, punitive amputations, live flayings. Detailed relief sculptures unearthed in the cities of Ninevah, Assur, Khorsabad, and Nimrud, along with bas-reliefs from royal palaces, had documented the torturous practices of the ancient Assyrians. Professor Fagan observed that these methods of torture had less to do with Assyrian cruelty than with the complexity of psychological warfare. In other words, inflicting unspeakable cruelty on a powerless people is an effective means of perpetuating subjugation. The conquered people internalize the cruelty so that it is no longer just their bodies that are subjugated, but also their minds. Professor Fagan was implying that there isn't anything monstrous about the institution of warfare. Rather, there is something monstrous about *us*.

Still in the newlywed spirit, Mitch and I murmured sweet pillow talk about how much we would love each other if we lived in ancient Assyria, and how, out of respect for me, Mitch would bring home neither severed hands nor heads to our small but attractive hut on the banks of the Tigris River. We fell asleep.

I woke abruptly to the full glare of the overhead light. Mitch was sitting in his skivvies on the edge of the bed, holding a Generation IV .40-caliber semiautomatic Glock. He pulled back the slide rail and chambered a round. The click bit the silence and my heart dropped.

I sat bolt upright, fully awake. "What is it?"

"Somebody's in the house. Stay here. Lock the door behind me."

"How do you know? I don't hear anything." Now I was swiftly getting dressed. It was 3:23 a.m.

"The front doors are standin wide open."

"Both of them?"

We kept one of the double doors dead-bolted to the jamb, using the other for daily comings and goings.

"Wide open, both of them."

"Could they have blown open?" A December wind was tossing the wind chimes.

"With Dad checkin the doors all the time?"

"Don't kill anybody," I said.

"If somebody's in this house, he's goin down."

"Shoot him in the knee," I suggested. "You could just *disable* him."

He looked at me as if I had said something incomprehensibly off-topic. Pulling the door shut behind him, he vanished down the hall.

I dropped like a child to my knees beside the bed and began to pray that there would be no shooting. Then I decided I'd better check on Albert, so I cracked the door and stuck my head into the hall. It didn't *feel* scary. Wouldn't your intuition tell you when there was a burglar in your house? The wind was blowing in particles of icy sleet through the open double doors, and the rug was getting wet. The cat was sleeping undisturbed in his favorite chair. Nothing appeared to be missing. What would a burglar want from a house like ours? We didn't have a TV.

And why would a burglar want to burgle in weather like this? I shut and bolted the front doors. Then I listened at Albert's bedroom. He was snoring.

I met Mitch coming up the stairs. He was still in his skivvies, but he had found my pink zip-up running jacket and put it on, the fuchsia stretched tight, the open zipper framing his muscular chest. He was still holding the Glock in front of him. I said, "Right now you'd be perfect on a float in an LGBT parade."

He didn't think it was funny. "Get back in the bedroom," he said shortly. "Don't come out until I say so."

I retreated, but I wasn't scared anymore. When he finally came to bed, reporting that the house was secure, he didn't melt against me as he usually did. He didn't sigh and rub his scratchy chin on my cheek, or roll his heavy thigh over mine. Instead he lay stiff as whipcord. Eventually he put his arm around me and drew my head down to his chest, but even as I drifted off, I heard his heart's thunder, too loud, gathering like a distant storm.

In the morning Albert confirmed that he had indeed checked the locks before retiring—many times, he said. He performed this useful service every five minutes, so we didn't doubt it. Together Mitch and I checked the locks on the front doors. Everything seemed to be working properly. The interlude was a mystery until, later that day when I was dusting Albert's living room, the double doors opened so violently that they slammed the walls. A powerful gust of ice-cold wind stirred the curtains. On closer scrutiny I saw that the over-the-door wreath holder had somehow disabled the lock. Operator error, as usual! The yuletide wreath on the front door had been my contribution. It had never occurred to me that my festive wreath, a symbol of goodwill and hospitality, might put us in harm's way.

I stood there a moment in the entrance, the doors still wide open, as if we welcomed all comers. Albert, behind me in his easy chair, hadn't heard the doors slam back, but now he felt the cold. "Rhoda, is that you? Did the doors blow open again? We don't want to heat the world!"

Unwilling to let the wreath go, I took down the over-the-door hook and bolted the door once more to the jamb. Then I went and got a hammer and a nail and pounded the latter directly into the wood of the door. The wreath looked fine this way, even better. The homey plaid bow and the clusters of pretty ornaments said, "Come in, come in, make yourself at home!" I imagined a burglar sneaking up to our house in the dark, maybe a kid driven by a white-hot habit, as Mitch had been once. I imagined him loosening a screen, breaking a window. He'd find my jewelry box, empty my sparkling rings into his pockets. He'd have my laptop under one arm, and he'd be moving fast, hurrying against the clock, against the Glock, against the cool deliberation that might be waiting for him in the shadow of the hall.

Drama is as curious in presence as it is in absence. It comes and goes with its own strange violence, like those whorls of snow that suddenly occlude the road, rising one moment, dissipating the next. Life seems somehow too ordinary when the drama is over.

That night after Mitch got home from work, he took me and Leroy out for ice cream. In the Christmas season I usually prefer a nice mug of spiced mulled cider, but my men cling to their Coffee Lover's Dream and Tommy Turtles no matter the weather. Dressed in parkas and knit hats, we went to the drive-through at Captain Sundae. Then we ate our ice cream in the car, the heat on full blast.

Leroy had been at his mother's for the weekend; we hadn't told him about our scare in the middle of the night. Therefore his question came interestingly, but relevantly, out of left field. "Hey Dad," he said from the backseat. "Which celebrity would you fight?"

Mitch answered with zero hesitation, as if he'd given the matter prior thought. "Pierce Brosnan. Charlie Sheen. Tom Cruise. David Spade. In that order." He dipped a thoughtful spoon into his ice cream and added, "Pierce Brosnan needs an atomic elbow to the kidney."

We were a blended family, so I strove to blend. "I'll fight Winona Ryder, the Pillsbury Doughboy, and Mr. Peanut. But not at the same time."

Leroy endorsed my list, but said sorrowfully that he couldn't fight a woman.

"Sure you can," I encouraged. "Because your hands and feet are tied, and all you can do is spit."

Leroy said in that case Winona Ryder was going down.

Mitch added, "Who's that lady from *Little Missy on the Prairie*? Elizabeth Gilbert. I think I could take her."

"You mean *Melissa* Gilbert," I said helplessly.

"There ain't no call to dress up like it's 1865."

"Then I take it you oppose Civil War reenactments?" I asked. "The cannons, the musketry, the charge of battle?"

Leroy hooted in derision. "Dorksquad!"

Mitch clutched his shoulder and lurched backward in his seat. His southern accent deepened: "A ball has lodged in my shoulder, sir! Ah think Ah'm done for! Permission to clip a lock of hair from my head and send it to my wife, sir!"

Leroy, too, lurched backward. "Permission to die of rocket diarrhea and head lice, sir!"

"Dysentery," I corrected. "Civil War reenactments can be educational."

"Tom Cruise be groomin his whiskers, pretendin like he got an important message from Robert E. Lee."

It had never occurred to me that straight men might consider playacting unmanly, yet clearly this was so. The merry scorn of my husband and son also explained their hypothetical willingness to fight Hollywood celebrities, who playacted for a living. I sighed.

"Gentlemen," I said, "has it ever occurred to you that an atomic elbow to the kidney might not be the best way to settle disputes?"

They laughed. Mitch said, "Tell you what. You sit down and talk it out with Mr. Peanut and Mr. Peanut's lawyer. But when somebody's in your house, all that talkin won't protect you."

Leroy offered me a spoonful of hot fudge. "You know what's really weird?"

"What?"

"That you guys get along so good. Because, don't take this the wrong way, sometimes you seem like you're from different planets."

I did my best alien imitation. "I come in peace," I said.

"I come with an atomic elbow," said Mitch.

"I come with a Tommy Turtle," said Leroy.

This was as true and as sweet as ice cream in December. We each had our different priorities. If you held them lightly and used a plastic spoon, they were nothing to get stuck on.

TWELVE

Double Dip

For readers who don't get what the Mennonites are all about,
I refer you to my last book, *Mennonite in a Little Black
Dress*. This has a helpful appendix. But if you are the sort of
reader who says, "Aww, Geez," at the thought of an appendix,
allow me to sum up Mennonite praxis in a pleasant haiku.
What's more fun than trying to squeeze five hundred years of
Anabaptist theology into a poem the size of a Chiclet?

If you are like me, you will admire this excellent exercise
in brevity. In the nineteenth century schoolmarms often made
their charges rewrite a 1,000-word theme as 500 words, then
250, then 100. The lesson, so American, was, Find your point
and own it. May I suggest that we all try to distill the essence of
our group, denomination, or sect into seventeen syllables?

I'll get the ball rolling with a haiku for the Mennonites. Attention, readers! We need to hear from Moslems, Jews, Baha'is,
and Hindus, not to mention Mormons, Methodists, atheists,
and those folks who think they're channeling helpful entities
from the Great Beyond. We can omit the *kigo*, the seasonal ref-

erence standard in haiku, on the grounds that religion is for all seasons. In fact you could say that religion is timeless, not unlike a little black dress.

Mennonite Haiku

Jesus lived in peace.

Let's give it a try! It helps

to have hot prune soup.

In the Radical Reformation of the sixteenth century Mennonites were called *Anabaptists*, which literally means "do over on the baptism." Menno Simons and other early Anabaptist leaders taught that baptism was a meaningless sign unless you did it as a personal choice. Because babies couldn't make choices, the Anabaptists refused to baptize infants. This refusal was interpreted by the Catholic authorities as an eloquent middle finger.

When I first heard about the origins of the Mennonite church, I couldn't understand why the Mennonites needed to be so rigid. If infant baptism was a meaningless sign, why not do it and make the authorities happy? Couldn't you decide to get rebaptized again as a grown-up? Mennonites seeking baptism were supposed to be fully conscious of the significance of the act as a public declaration of filiation with Christ. But I didn't see why you couldn't add some judicious baby-sprinkling too.

As a young girl I therefore sprinkled like a yard butler, baptizing myself at every opportunity. No body of water was safe from my holy crusade. I baptized myself in the Tub-o'-the-Dead, in Lola's Doughboy pool, even in the irrigation trenches in the orchard. Was I deterred if I scooped up a tadpole or a dead peeper? By no means! The peeper I presented to God as evidence of Christian piety, and I poured the frog onto my brow with a noble shudder. When poor Hannah was old enough to be bullied into baptizing me, no game was complete without a concluding moment in which she pronounced me sanctified in the name of the Father, the Son, and the Holy Ghost.

One Sunday evening our church hosted a traveling missionary who "had a heart for the nations," in the parlance of Sunday School teachers. At first I assumed this phrase meant that the missionary wanted to tell people in different countries about Jesus. But it turned out that he just wanted to scare the pants off us. This missionary was all about hellfire and brimstone. The congregation of decorous worshippers must have thought "!!!!!," because in my church of origin Mennonites did not preach about hell. We believed in it. But we preferred not to talk about it. It was bad manners to talk about hell.

Sometimes my mother made me go over and play badminton with Pam Bedrosian, the loud neighbor girl whose horsey laugh I dreaded. At eight years old, she had the most hirsute arms I had ever seen, and also a promising black moustache. With her plastic ponies and her meaty cartwheels, Pam expressed zero interest in baptism. Nonetheless my mother occasionally packed up some fresh apple *pereshki* for Mrs. Bedrosian and hustled me out the door. "Make sure you stay long enough to be polite!"

"Awww, Mom, Pam belches the alphabet in Armenian."

"Pam is in touch with her Armenian heritage."

"But she *belches* her heritage. Every time. In a big loud voice."

"Belchers need friends too."

I knew there would be a spanking if I refused to pay homage to Pam and her heritage. Thus I experienced many an afternoon of Good Samaritan badminton. Pam may have been the sort of rip-roaring, milk-snorting child to turn her eyelids out, but she wasn't fooled for a moment. She knew that I didn't want to play badminton, or ponies, or Sasquatch, or walk down to the 7-Eleven to check for quarters under the vending machines. The only reason I was at the Bedrosian residence at all was to escape punishment.

God probably felt the same way when people converted just to avoid hell.

So I was not expecting the traveling preacher to address the topic of the lake of burning fire. (Is there any other kind of fire?) This missionary preacher had found his topic of choice, and he warmed to it. He spoke passionately about hell, as if he had been there and might be interested in going back. His enthusiasm reminded me of my brothers, who, when they came across something gross such as dog poop, really wanted me to know and share their revulsion, and thus might present it to me on a cracker. This missionary's sole reason for seeking the loving arms of Jesus was to avoid the miseries of hell.

The sermon described a fiery vista involving the fallen Lucifer, his minions, the sinners of the ages moaning in said lake of burning fire, and a pack of slavering wild dogs. Although the missionary preacher did not expressly say so, I assumed that these slavering dogs were fanged like chupacabras. Whence came the hellhounds into a Mennonite sermon I do not know. Maybe the missionary had read Milton. At the time I had not read Milton, and so I accepted the chupacabras without question. Cats being my pet of choice, it didn't surprise me one bit that the epicenter of all feral dog activity was hell, and that sinners would be hanging out with sorcerers, idolaters, whoremongers, and chupacabras.

The missionary instructed us to consider the worst personal torture we could imagine, and then to project that torture into our mental image of hell. My slavering dogs instantly began to belch the alphabet in Armenian, and to cavort and gambol on the fiery shore of the lake of burning fire, there among the whoremongers. The dogs jumped and twisted and did powerful backflips, defying all natural laws. Some were writhing in flames like the Anabaptists in the *Martyrs' Mirror*. Say what you will, but there is something monstrous about an eructating dog that turns aerial cartwheels.

I called my mother to ask if she remembered this missionary and his punitive message, which I might sum up as: "Say Uncle, Sinner!"

"You're sure this fellow was Mennonite? Mennonites don't scare people into salvation."

"I don't remember if he was Menno or what, only that he spoke at our church. Like Jonathan Edwards but with feral dogs."

"Once at a Lutheran church where Si was speaking we saw a children's feature. It started off as a sweet puppet show. What do you call those puppets on strings?"

"Marionettes."

"The puppet show was about the Second Coming. When Jesus came, half the puppets were suddenly whisked up to heaven, and all the children started crying. One little boy was just screaming in terror."

Unlike the Lutheran screamer, I was old enough to keep my new fear to myself. A sense of gathering doom began to rise, like waters around Noah's ark. A sea of vast, unnamable foreboding swirled beneath conscious thought. All would be well if I could make it to adulthood, but what if I died young, in a tragic volcano accident like Krakatoa? What if I died because of a deadly peanut allergy, as with Matt Bash? Matt Bash was someone I *knew*, sort of. My hours of baptismal ablutions had been a warm-up for the real thing, but not the thing itself, like practice before a game. Hannah looked like a wee angel with her white hair and blue eyes, but she was no John the Baptist. In fact she was technically not old enough to count as a believer, since she did anything you told her to do, such as scattering rose petals in front of you as you walked. No: I needed the real deal, the holy dip, the total dunk, in the name of the triune God.

I don't know how long I lived in fear of the slavering dogs. Weeks of nightmares, stories, drawings, and homemade amulets ensued. I chanted and incanted; I prayed and genuflected, like Catholic Alice Bash. The tension increased. One day at Pam Bedrosian's house I burst into tears and wouldn't stop. "Crybaby!" shouted Pam. "Baby has a soft spot! Baby has a fontanelle! If you don't say why you're crying this minute, I'm going to hit you in the head as hard as I can with this shuttlecock!"

She did so, with splendid precision.

At bedtime my mother finally managed to pry the fear out of me, and I lay sobbing across her lap. Hiccoughing with relief, I told her that all this could be avoided if only Mennonites would practice child baptism.

My mother, bless her, did what she could to reassure me. Hadn't I accepted Jesus into my heart? Then I would surely be going to heaven! She unbraided my tight braids and massaged my temples and kissed me good night. Hannah was already asleep in her single bed, and the rhythmic rising and falling of her breath in the dark underscored the vulnerability of childhood. We were young, we were weak, we could be squashed like spiders. What could I do but take my chances? Loved but unbaptized!

I stiffened. A sober, preacherly knock.

Bedtime comforts were the office of my mother. I had never seen my father in my bedroom before, except to administer a spanking after a protracted time-out. But here he was in the flesh, handsome and crew cut, tall and terrifying. He sat down on the edge of my bed and cleared his throat. "I hear you're interested in baptism."

I nodded, sitting up against the pillow and folding my hands over my flannel nightie. "I don't want to go to hell. I don't like dogs that belch."

"I seeeeeeee." He rubbed his chin in his hand, as if following a complex but subtle argument.

"I might die before I grow up and get baptized," I said in a rush. "Lots of people do. Alice Bash's brother died and then grade four got him a bench."

"A bench?"

"In his memory. They put it by the principal's office, but nobody is allowed to sit on it."

"A decorative bench. Go on."

"Except that Matt Bash was Catholic, so he went to heaven. Matt Bash was baptized. I'm not. If I died, I would go to hell."

"I think I can help you." My father was opening his Bible to the Gospel of Luke. And in a steady voice with no trace of humor, he read aloud the story of the two criminals who were crucified next to Jesus. One criminal mocks Jesus, but the other asks to be remembered when Jesus enters into his Kingdom. Jesus answers, "Truly I say to you, today you shall be with me in Paradise." My father went on to explain the concept of precedence. If this criminal could go to heaven without baptism, then so could I. The criminal would have gotten baptized if he had lived, just as I would get baptized when I became an adult. But because of the extenuating circumstances, Jesus made an exception. He would for me too, if I died before I grew up.

Oh, the comfort! How grateful I was that my father did not try to reassure me that I wouldn't die young, or that the hounds of hell were not necessarily a part of the biblical landscape! This conversation with my father was the best dad moment of my childhood. I remember it as the first time my father and I interacted person to person, the first time he looked at me and saw a real mind with real sorrow, troubled, like all humanity, by equations of cause and effect.

So helpful were my father's comments that I soon released Hannah from her baptism duties. By the time I was old enough to participate in the church's youth group, I no longer cared about baptism. I cared about Max Factor Kissing Potion. Max

Factor Kissing Potion made the lips very shiny and it came in a flavor called Chocolate Fudge. But after twenty minutes on the mouth, the potion developed a thin unattractive crust that ringed the interior of the lips. This white residue recalled the sleep in the corner of your eye when you woke up in the morning. It was the opposite of sexy, yet you couldn't achieve cultural currency without risking White Line Fever. All the girls at school wore Max Factor Kissing Potion, even me. I kept mine in my locker where my mother would not find it. It was with relief and a real sense of maturity that I joined the sisterhood of watchers who might stop one another in the hall between classes and whisper, "Fever, girl. You're burning up." Ah, we are never too young to learn that beauty requires constant vigilance!

As soon as I was old enough, I would embrace the world that lay waiting after high school—college, miniskirts, coffeehouses. Finally I would understand why they served espresso with a little twist of lemon! All matters of the spirit were swept under the rug because I had now graduated from the church library to the public library.

My mother allowed me to take armloads of books, with a limit of twenty-five in one week. She assumed that I was consuming age-appropriate material, but I was not. I read Nancy Drew alongside Jacqueline Susann's *Valley of the Dolls*. I was not trying to be either retro or worldly. I just didn't know better. Therefore I became the Tasmanian devil of indiscriminate reading. It would be lovely to blame my frenzied childhood reading patterns on severe Mennonite underexposure, but the truth is that some little girls are destined to read in elevators for a good twenty-five minutes before remembering that they have forgotten to select a floor.

Nineteenth-century novels with heroines falling through the ice: What's not to love? Phaetons and reticules were obviously a thing of the past, but some things, such as tender deathbed adieux, were surely timeless. I didn't understand that many of the books offered nostalgic nods to bygone eras. Teen novels of the forties and fifties, like *Class Ring* and *Boy Trouble*, prepared me to expect well-scrubbed youths who would ask to carry my books and walk me home from a malt shop. Gee whiz, that'd be terrif! Nor did I know that Karl Marx was a surprising read for a thirteen-year-old. Religion, opiate of the people! Heavy petting, downfall of youth!

When I was thirteen, church was like a painfully uncool grape tray on which you had been forced to decoupage a poster of a kitten saucily batting a Christmas-tree light, beneath which an artiste had written in calligraphy John 8:12:

I am the light of the world.

Having rejected both kittens and Christ, I certainly did not want this grape tray in my room, but my mother said that since I had made it at a youth group activity, I should keep it hanging round for a while.

I was not keen on dating Mennonite boys, but I didn't know any other kind. Not that I could actually date. Dating was a promise that, like the espresso, beckoned from a mysterious future. However, not even an embarrassing Dorothy Hamill haircut could stop me from flirting.

Rodney Regier, aged sixteen, was the Ambassador of Ambiguity. On the one hand he snapped my bra strap and kept me talking about *Atlas Shrugged* twenty minutes after youth group was over. On the other, he hung around Libby Arndt, who ran with the college crowd. Libby was sixteen too, but she had an older brother at Fresno Pacific who taught her about clove cigarettes and Ed Ruscha. Lola, my best friend then as now, also had older, cooler siblings, and she had attended one of Libby's parties. These events, often themed, were much discussed in Mennonite youth circles. They came together with spectacular speed and efficiency, as soon as Libby's parents left town.

Lola described the function she attended as an unqualified success. All guests had been instructed to wear black and white. The hostess greeted them at the door in a thrift-store blouse from Farrell's. Farrell's was a fake Gay Nineties ice cream parlor where female servers dressed up as Gibson Girls. The Gibson Girls wore black-and-white pinstriped blouses with enormous signature leg-o'-mutton sleeves. Even I knew that Farrell's was hopelessly uncool. Thus Libby's lambchop sleeves represented a subversive gesture, a declaration of true fashion brio. And it was all the more stunning because Libby was built like a dorm-room refrigerator. You had to give it up for a girl shaped like Stonehenge who had the cheek to wear sleeves that puffed out a good foot beyond the shoulder.

The guests had watched *Roi de Coeur, King of Hearts*, against a backdrop of badass patchouli incense. They had sipped what they considered a lubricious cosmopolitan cocktail involving Pernod and absinthe. Libby could have arranged opium hookahs if she'd had a mind to. She ordered people around like a French film director. Always she was the one who had it supremely together, the one who could make everybody rethink the mutton chop. In the middle of a church youth group meeting Libby might rise and move into a pretend spotlight, where she'd declaim dramatically, "A dingo ate my baaaaaaybee!" When Libby said it, you felt that dingoes were the stuff of timeless soliloquies.

To this day I wonder why Libby wanted Rodney. Maybe she didn't. Maybe she just gathered up folks as she swept along because she could. It didn't surprise anybody, except maybe Libby's parents, when Libby grew up to reject the church. She was known for her outspoken criticisms in that area for a while. Then she stopped caring about the Mennonites and went on to become a very successful life coach. My friend Grace, a lapsed Mennonite who knew Libby in college, once contacted Libby to see if maybe Libby would consider being her life coach. Libby's professional fee was high, but she had a great reputation in the field. Her website invited applicants to summarize their situation in five hundred words or fewer. Grace did so, taking the full five hundred words to say, "I am a mess, my family is a mess, my marriage is a mess, and I can't seem to move forward even though I am aware of my flaws." Grace and I were stunned by the prompt reply. Libby declined Grace's application. In her brusque note of rejection, Libby intimated that Grace was too much of a mess.

"I thought a life coach's clients were *supposed* to be a mess," I said. "Else why would they need a life coach in the first place?"

"I can't believe I'm too much of a mess for even a life coach!" Grace exclaimed. "Geez!"

"Maybe you should try a whole new approach," I said. "How about you quit your job and become a life coach?"

Two or three years later Grace thought she remembered someone at a party mentioning that Libby had passed away rather suddenly of leukemia. This news coincided with my own cancer downtick, so I pressed Grace for details. But Grace couldn't remember who had told her that Libby was dead. I Googled Libby. Her webpage was no longer up, but that in itself didn't confirm the rumor. So I called my mom to ask if she knew whether Libby was dead.

"Who's Libby Arndt?"

"Abe and Agnes Arndt's oldest daughter. Remember, she published some essays criticizing the church in the eighties? Libby married Jump-or-Dive Jeff Ratzlaff in college. They got a divorce a couple years later. Then she married a Baha'i guy who sold Herbalife."

"Jeff's father had a head shaped like a violin," my mother said.

"I have no response to that."

"Libby, Libby Arndt. No. I don't know if she's dead or what. I'll tell you who's dead. Libby Wiebe is dead. Renee Funk Wagner's daughter."

"Really? What'd she die of?"

"Breast cancer. She was just a couple years younger than you."

My mother and I shared a moment of silence for the long chill hand of death. Then she said brightly, "By the way, did you get the walnuts I sent?"

⌒

Thus I am unable to confirm whether my old nemesis is dead or alive. If it is the former, Rest in peace, dear Libby, blazer of trails, buster of chops, purveyor of vitamins! If it is the latter, Libby might like to know that Rodney became a church-planter in Asunción. When he finally returned to the States, he refused to let his four homeschooled daughters go to college. I'm thinking someone could use a life coach.

When Libby set her sights on something, she got it. Therefore the Rodney situation called for drastic measures. I signed up for the Butler Mennonite Brethren Church baptismal class. With their Anabaptist roots, Mennonites took baptism seriously. You couldn't just hustle people into choir robes and then plunge them into the baptistry willy-nilly. You had to make sure they were ready for this important rite. Were they choosing this step with full understanding and adult sentience, as demonstrated by John the Baptist in the Bible? Were they walking with the Lord? Were they prepared to give a public testimony, describing their journey with Jesus? When I heard that Rodney would be taking the baptism class, I thought, Score! Hours and hours with Rodney, and not a leg-o'-mutton in sight!

I did not feel bad about pretending to prioritize God. Having recently read Niccolò Machiavelli, I felt that, all things considered, the end did justify the means. Besides, I wasn't opposed to baptism per se. It was all very well, and someday I would be glad that I had done it, like the time I jumped off the high dive for a dime.

The Sunday evening before the actual baptism all the candidates had to present their testimonies to the church congregation. For most of my friends this was a dreaded ordeal. I've heard over and over that the number one fear of most adults is public speaking. Me, I would rather speak in public than sell vitamins or be a life coach, but so it goes. At thirteen I could proceed to the front of a classroom and deliver a presentation without stammering or consulting my notes. In the middle of it I might even begin to use the blackboard, explaining points and managing discussion. This is because eggheads are born, not made. However, I also liked to entertain a theory communicated to me by my Aunt Martha, who worked in a locked psychiatric facility for the chronically mentally ill. She once told me about a patient who went about day after day with his mouth hanging wide open, jaw slack, tongue loose. Finally one day she asked him why his mouth was always open. "It's so the angel can see out," he explained. I loved the idea of a busy angel of elocution who would dip one's words in gold.

Thus I expected not to mind the public testimony in front of four hundred people. Sunday night when my turn came to step in front of the mike, I looked out at the familiar faces, eager and supportive and kind. I knew I could lie about my faith to these fine people. In a moment I would be checked, but not by my own dishonesty.

The pastor asked me the same question he had asked all the others: "Rhoda, can you tell us a little bit about how you came to the Lord?"

I nodded confidently and accepted the mike. Suddenly, out of nowhere, a heaviness descended, palpable and dense as thick-napped velvet. This was a tight, personal heaviness that settled on my head like a hat, rather like the heaviness I felt during my wedding to Mitch thirty years later. I paused to take a breath.

The congregation smiled at what they must have thought was nervous-Nellie jitters.

Now the heaviness felt like a coat, a mantle. I turned and shrugged, but it followed me. It wouldn't shake off. It was tight, I tell you, and vaguely terrifying. In real confusion I hung my head—was I sick, did I have stage fright? But I knew what this was even as I asked the question. My Dorothy Hamill hairdo flopped forward with wings, like a panty shield. I hid behind my hair because I was ashamed. To the congregation I uttered one or two colorless sentences, parroting what the others had said.

This was the first time I experienced an inkling of the awesome reality of God with something like adult awareness. After the service I ran and hid in a stall in the ladies' lounge, as I often did when avoidant. Sitting still on the toilet, I struggled with the badness of what I had done, and what I was about to do the following Sunday in the baptistry. I was like the Apostle Peter in reverse, pretending to know Christ when I didn't. In came two high-heeled women talking about the service, clickety-click.

"I like your pocketbook," said one woman. "Is that mother-of-pearl?"

"It's just white tortoiseshell. I got it on sale at Gottschalk's. That Rodney Regier is sure on fire for the Lord."

"What a shame the Janzen girl doesn't have her father's gift for speaking."

"Girls are shy at that age."

There was the sound of aerosol hairspray: "Tsssst!"

The following Sunday morning I stood in the baptistry tank, doubly wrapped in two choir robes for the sake of modesty. A robed deacon passed me down the stairs, where the water came up to my chest. It sloshed and echoed under the bright lights. Above the baptistry, glass blocks filtered light in the shape of a cross, and I turned my eyes down, toward the water.

"Rhoda Janzen, do you confess Jesus Christ as your personal Savior?"

"I do."

"Then I baptize you in the name of the Father, the Son, and the Holy Ghost."

As the waters closed above me, I thought, "Tsssst!"

Man is a puff of air, his days a fleeting shadow. How can we not turn from this awful truth? Two months later I would be crushing on a different boy. I promptly dismissed the heavy feeling, not by rationalizing it, but by ignoring it utterly.

A couple of weeks ago I was sitting on the edge of the pool at the Holland Aquatic Center, resting after a class. As you know by now, I'm a runner by choice, not a swimmer. The rigors of chemo call for adaptability. Although my cancer is in remission, I'm still on an oral chemo program that weakens the bones and makes running painful. If you know someone who is passionate about running, you may recognize the *sui generis* refusal to stop. We're the type of person who, when the doctor tells us we have blown out our knee and require surgery, might lean forward and respond politely, "No, you don't understand, I'm a *runner*." Luckily my knees are holding as I advance into middle age. However, there's not much you can do when your ankles crisp up like pretzels. Chemo weakens the infrastructure.

Correction: there is plenty you can do, as Lola reminded me

on her last visit. You just have to be willing to try something new, even if you are dead certain that you will hate the new thing. Like Albert, I resist change. I didn't want to swim. I wanted to run. I'm a *runner*, see. I know it sounds ridiculous that this became a matter of prayer for me, but it was psychic torture to swap out two running days a week for two days of water aerobics. I missed the rush of endorphins, the pounding of feet on gravel, the sound of cicadas and chickadees. These things seem downright personal after running the first couple miles. My second wind usually hits around the fifty-minute mark, and after that it's all otherworldly bliss. So I was praying for the flexibility to enjoy a different sport. If you could call water aerobics a sport. Which I didn't.

More evidence that there is a God! Nothing but divine intervention could have provided the Waterlilies. The Holland Aquatic Center offered lots of aerobics classes, but this 7:00 a.m. one was the only one that fit my work schedule. I showed up with a crappy old swimsuit and a heart of resentment. Right on time, I wondered why the class had already started. Ah, they were seniors! Fifteen silver-haired heads were advancing slowly across the lanes, doing some kind of hurdle movement that was supposed to strengthen the core.

Turns out that these Waterlilies had been meeting twice a week for *twenty-six years*. The oldest was Pearl, who had been married to the same guy for sixty-seven years. Before I could even get in the water, the Lilies had all called out greetings and invitations to join them for breakfast at Southside. At the breakfast they passed around pictures of Minnie's great-grandson, a plump ten-month-old for whom the Lilies had thrown a deluxe baby shower. "The Lilies really stepped it up with baby clothes and diapers," Minnie explained. "My granddaughter, the baby's mother, isn't married."

"All the more reason to show support!" said Eunice, and the other Lilies nodded.

The Lilies looked terrific. From this I inferred that the hurdle movements really did strengthen the core, and so I gave it the old college try. Lola was right: water aerobics involved a real workout. That is, the cardio hurdles were a real workout. My favorite part of the class was the stretching at the end. Edie, the svelte seventysomething teacher, spaced us all out along a rope and played fifties music while we lifted one arm above our heads, ballerina style. We turned our wrists to and fro, this way and that, like game-show hostesses gesturing toward a handsome Winnebago. Vanna White should be so graceful!

Then we performed a series of movements from an era of fitness that once bejiggled cellulite with a vibrating belt. We held swimming noodles elegantly aloft while extending one leg forward. We made a giant lotus with our legs touching in the middle, like synchronized swimmers. We perfected a water do-si-do. Many of the movements had an air of distant elegance, as from the languid choreography of the Rainbow Room or the Carousel Club. Even if I had been allowed to dance as a young-ster, my dances would have been the Cabbage Patch, the Electric Slide, and the Macarena. Luckily I got points for knowing the Italian lyrics to "Volare."

And I thought nothing could ever match the pleasures of running!

Sitting there on the third step, inhaling the wonderfully satisfying smell of chlorine, I meditated on the healing properties of water. No wonder religion had co-opted water for its rites of passage. It rocked us in the cradle of the deep, speaking to the subconscious mind about transformation and change.

And that's when it occurred to me that maybe I should act like an Anabaptist and get rebaptized—now that I finally meant it. My pastor said once that if a person wasn't seeking God with his whole heart, baptism would mean nothing. It would slide right off like so many drops of water. A person with specious or lackluster faith would descend into the water as a fake and would emerge as a fake, end of story. In the many years since my teenage baptism, things had changed. Now I could honestly get up in front of a roomful of people and say, "Hey everybody. When I was thirteen, I phoned this in. I got baptized for a guy with an overbite. And so today I'm doing it all over again, because now I can do it with a right heart. You're my church family. Over the last two years I've listened to your stories and I've watched your lives. They've proven to me that change is possible. My old life wasn't cutting it anymore, so thank you for showing me something different."

I figured if God had brought me to the water, it might be a hint, the kind even I might notice. Perhaps God would be open to giving the youngest Waterlily some guidance in the matter of getting rebaptized? After that everything began to rain down baptism—daily devotions, favorite theologians, snippets of overheard conversations.

Pretty soon I didn't even need the cosmic hints. I'd bend over to check out a hotspot on my foot, going, "Why would a pair of comfy flip-flops with soft cloth flowers be giving me a blister?" And the Poovey voice would say, "A BAPTISM won't give you a blister!"

"Will this grit-and-cheese soufflé be enough for five people?"

"Perhaps, as long as one of them is BAPTIZED."

"Does this skirt make me look like Agnolo the Fat?"

"Yes, but unlike you, Agnolo the Fat was BAPTIZED."

One night I said to Mitch, "Do you think it would be okay to get rebaptized?"

"Yes! Do it!"

"If you think I should, then why didn't you say something?"

"Baptism needs to come from the belly. Ain't no sense puttin suggestions into people's minds. You don't get baptized because other people think you should. You get baptized because you feel the hand of God on your life."

Unlike the Mennonites, the Pentecostals don't insist on a long class. They offer a service every couple of months, and anybody can sign up. It was on a Saturday when I first shared my interest in baptism with Mitch. That evening we made a promise to God. When God got around to sending the opportunity, I'd jump on it. It felt terrific to have formalized my intention in front of God and husband.

The very next day, in the Sunday evening service, the pastor began to preach about the various kinds of baptism that the Bible talks about. I was thinking, "So okay, God, stop with the hints already! I read you loud and clear! I *said* I'd get baptized, what more do you want?"

Suddenly the pastor stood stock still, as Pentecostals do from time to time. They like to be open to spontaneous moves of God. It always reminds me of when a big dog hears something inaudible to the human ear, like the toot sweet in *Chitty Chitty Bang Bang*. "I'm feeling by the Holy Spirit that we should have a baptism soon," the pastor exclaimed. Clearly this was news to him. He took a few paces, as if wrestling with a knotty problem. "In fact tonight! Right now! I'm feeling by the Spirit that someone here wants to be baptized. Is there anybody here who desires to be baptized?"

My hand shot up so fast I didn't even see the nine other people who raised their hands too, like kids eager to be called on.

And so I got to say what I wanted to say. Once more I stood in a double choir robe in a chilly tank of water. I was the first. Below the baptistry the congregation was standing and clapping to support the ten of us. My husband's earnest gaze was saying either "Praise God Almighty" or "Tighten up that choir robe." This time I had ditched the Dorothy Hamill 'do, and my hair was pulled into a tasteful twist. There in the baptismal tank I happily accepted the microphone.

When I opened my mouth to speak, it wasn't to Mitch, grateful as I was to the man who had shown me hour by hour the peace of applied faith. I was speaking to the whole church, to all people of faith everywhere. I was speaking to all the people whose lives had encouraged me to step out of my comfort zone. The encouragement hadn't come from their mouths. It had come from their actions, from the way they lived. All my life I had been so busy criticizing organized religion that I hadn't actually taken stock of what was happening around me. People on the spiritual path were seeking and finding peace. They were the ones who, in allowing themselves to be changed, became more effective at loving others.

Baptism is supposed to be a sign of the individual belief of the person rocking the two wet choir robes. And in a way it was, because how could I miss the symmetry? The second ceremony extended rather than corrected the first. Taken together, both ceremonies argued that we need to acknowledge denial and self-absorption in order to move beyond them.

An hour before church I had watched a YouTube clip of a makeup artist demonstrating how to do an intensely smoky seventies eye. "This is a fresh look when you update the colors for today," said the makeup artist. "Just sweep the pale mocha cream shadow across the lid and then blend!" Right after the video I'd experimented with this look myself, repeating into the mirror, "Just sweep the pale mocha cream shadow across the lid and then get BAPTIZED!" Now, standing damp as a muskrat in the water, I began to cry. I was peacefully unaware that an effluvium of eye shadow was coursing down my face, like something from *Mommie Dearest*. But you know what? I wouldn't have cared even if I had remembered the blended symphony of mocha and taupe.

I clung to my pastor's hand as he and an elder brought me into and then out of the water. On the stairs waited the other nine. A few were already holding the rails, standing in the water. I didn't know my fellow baptismal candidates very well—there were some beautifully excited high schoolers, a pop-n-lock young break-dancer who could really bust a move, a guy who repeatedly went forward to get prayer for healing, and a mother whose kids I sometimes watched in the church nursery. Joy in their faces, joy in their hands. They reached out to help me up the stairs. In the water their choir robes lifted and swirled like the stories that follow us all.

ACKNOWLEDGMENTS

Every day I say out loud that I am grateful for my family and friends, so it gives me a special satisfaction to formalize my gratitude as part of a book project that wouldn't have happened without them. Maybe it's weird to say how much I love my editor, Helen Atsma, and my agent, Michael Bourret, since they're professional associates and all. But how lucky is this? I'd love them even if I had no professional reason to call on their wisdom, instinct, and skill. In fact I think the three of us should have a slumber party.

Special thanks to my colleagues at Hope College, especially David Klooster, my inspiration at work as in life. If I have grown as a teacher and writer, it's because he showed me how. English professors, of course, hang out with other English professors. So my girlfriends are in a unique position to give me writerly counsel and savvy feedback as well as birthday brownies and hand-knit hats. But I also want to thank them just for being their gorgeous, funny selves—Carla Vissers, Julie Kipp, Beth Trembley, and the late, much-missed Jenn Young. Special thanks to Laura Roberts, Susan Philips, and Anna-Lisa Cox, all of whom put the *courage* in *encourage*.

To my best friend, Jill Janzen, I humbly suggest that gals who have been best friends for forty-two years really ought to run off to Filicudi for a week or two. I know I should thank Jill for her insight, her creativity, her thereness, but what I really want to say is, Thank you for all those times we have laughed ourselves to tears, for instance that time in Palermo in the Jesus Pit. What a companion you have been, what a sister of the heart.

I am grateful to Joanne and Will Jenkins and their daughter Emma Jenkins. The former read my draft with her eagle eye and then whupped me at Scrabble. The latter taught me a new game: the Beef-a-Roo, also a popular dance step. Call me crazy, but *The Beef-a-Roo* might make a nice title for a novel!

Thanks to my parents, who, like my sister, read this in manuscript form. If anybody needs a marital model of faith applied to decades, check out the steadfast dearness of my mom and dad. After fifty-two years of marriage, they're still passing a tiny snake-bite kit back and forth, hiding it in unlikely places. That's not spiritually edifying per se, but it's pretty cute.

My new family has played the biggest supporting role in this project. Hugs to Korry and Holly and Elmer, and to my husband, TR, who reasonably asked me to change his name and place of residence for my last book. When I invited my stepson, Korry, to choose his own fictional name, Korry picked Leroy. Elmer said to stick with Albert. TR said that he feels more like a Benito than a Mitch, but he advised me to keep the latter since I had already used it. Now that TR and I are an old married couple, he's given me full permission to claim him as my man.

My husband's openness and candor have been inspiring. Whenever I asked him if I could write about such-and-such, he'd say, "Do it. Write it. What's the value of experience if we can't reflect on it?"

Finally, thanks to my pastor and church family for showing me, day by day, season after season, the communal power of prayer. How much I have learned, and still have to learn, from this joyful cloud of witnesses.

READING GROUP GUIDE

Questions for Discussion

1. Much of this memoir turns on the contrast between faith and intellect. Do you believe that the two are fundamentally incompatible? Does Rhoda?

2. The story frames breast cancer as a "lady problem," but the narrative implies that there are other far more significant lady problems. What are they? Does Rhoda suggest any solutions for these lady problems?

3. When Rhoda and her brother played the geography game, she stumped him by choosing Chad, a country so large and obvious that her brother wouldn't spot it. Have you ever had a blind spot the size of Chad in your life? What was it? What did it take for you to finally notice it?

4. Why does Rhoda use humor to downplay her struggle with cancer? At one point Rhoda suggests that, since childhood, she has struggled with avoidance. Is the cancer humor an example of avoidance? If so, what is Rhoda failing to confront? If not,

what positive function might the humor have? Can humor enable growth? Can it free us from fear?

5. Rhoda grew up in a sober Mennonite community, and she is surprised to find that the Pentecostals really know how to shake it. What other differences did you notice between Mennonite and Pentecostal services? Have you ever visited places of worship different from your own? Did your visit broaden your understanding of your faith?

6. Rhoda says that gratitude has become so important to her that she is willing to do almost anything to get more of it. In your experience, what are the positive outcomes of gratitude? Rhoda goes out of her way to practice feeling gratitude. How does she achieve it? Can anyone achieve it, or do you have to be predisposed to it? Can you think of any dangers inherent in the deliberate cultivation of gratitude?

7. Rhoda speaks of learning to put down past resentments and grudges. How has she achieved that? Have you ever been able to set down your biggest grudge, your all-time worst hurt? Can it be done without calling on a Higher Power?

8. When it comes right down to it, chapter eight, "The Gottman Island Survival Experience," is an argument for abstinence. What are the pros and cons of abstinence in contemporary American culture? How would your life have been different if you had (or had not) embraced abstinence before making a commitment to your partner?

9. Rhoda and Mitch wonder if other couples have been similarly impacted by the sacramental power of the marriage covenant. What do you think? Is the institution of marriage ultimately any different from a monogamous romantic partnership?

10. Chapter ten, "The Poovey Voice," suggests that spiritual seekers must learn to give before they will receive. Do you believe that financial giving is important to spiritual growth? What about other kinds of giving? Think of the greatest, hardest gift you have ever given; did it result in your growth?

11. Mitch admits that Albert does not love him "overmuch." Do you know any parents who do not love their children "overmuch"? Rhoda and Mitch believe that Albert's chronic negativity is harmful. How do they respond to it? What should adult children do when parents display unhealthy behavior? Is this the time for boundaries, or forgiveness?

12. Albert keeps all of his late wife's things. Rhoda says she believes in "a clean sweep" after a breakup or the death of a loved one. In what ways is Rhoda making "a clean sweep" after her first marriage? How is Mitch making a sweep of his own?

13. Rhoda is a poet who finds meaning in the laundry room wallpaper, whereas Albert prides himself on his ability to face facts. When Rhoda describes her mother's "merry heart," we recognize this same quality in Rhoda's approach to her life, even in hard times. Albert approaches his life with a darker outlook, priding himself in his ability to confront tough truths head-on.

What are the pros and cons of each perspective? What do Rhoda and Albert have to teach each other?

14. One of the most haunting moments of this book is when Albert recalls being visited by Billy's ghost. How does Albert's rational mind-set affect his response to this otherworldly experience? How would you explain the ghost?

15. How does Rhoda's parents' marriage shape her expectations for her own new marriage?

16. What role does faith play in Rhoda's relationship with Mitch? How does their relationship change from the beginning of the book to the end?

17. What does Rhoda learn from her church? How does her spiritual life grow and change over the course of this story? What did you take away from her journey?

A Conversation with Rhoda Janzen

Q: *What inspired you to write a second memoir?*
A: After I wrote *Mennonite in a Little Black Dress*, I was inundated with reader requests to keep writing. People overwhelmingly welcomed the idea of reframing difficult life experiences with humor and gratitude. And my life has changed so extraordinarily since then! I had much more to share.

Q: Glad to see your family is still such a strong part of your life, even when you're not living with your parents! How has your family grown with this new marriage? Were you surprised by your new role as daughter-in-law and stepparent?

A: Oh, my family continues to crack me up. Who wouldn't love cheapo senior parents who agree to housesit for a stranger on Craigslist in order to get a free coastal vacation? I asked my mom how it was and, always upbeat, she said, "Well, there was a friendly cat!"

The new family is fabulous. My eighty-one-year-old father-in-law treats his lady friends to Sunday dinner in the local hospital cafeteria because they have a nice pot roast for $6.99. And nothing keeps you flexible like a son who plays the ukulele and a daughter with inexplicable ink. One of her tattoos features a realistic wolf *en profile* in the middle of a Spirograph design. Do I get it? No! Can I get behind it? All the way!

Q: Do you believe your Mennonite upbringing instilled your sense of faith? What have you learned from the new Pentecostal community?

A: Ah, who can know what forces collude to pull us toward the divine? I do know that over the years my parents prayed for me, and I have come to believe in the power of prayer.

My new community has taught me many practical things. One of the best is the role of joyful praise. Outside, looking in, an observer might go, "Why are those folks so happy all the time?" But Pentecostal praise doesn't come from the emotions. It's a decision, an act of will, and as such it dramatically changes your notion of what it means to bless and be blessed.

Q: What's the funniest thing you've heard shouted in church?

A: First let me say that in my church of origin I never heard a peep, not a single "Amen!" Congregants sat in respectful silence, or, in my case, doodled in the bulletin. So I was delighted to find that Pentecostals will shout out anything at all, in noisy solidarity and goodwill.

Once my pastor was talking about cultural overchoice. To make his point, he brought in a box of breakfast cereal. He said, "I stood there in the cereal aisle, surrounded by option after option: Cheerios, Lucky Charms, Frosted Flakes, Wheaties—"

"I LIKE ME SOME WHEATIES!!!" shouted Sister Fanny.

I clapped hard for Fanny. Pentecostals also feel free to applaud, see.

Q: Are there any other memoirs about faith you'd like to recommend?

A: Sure. I read two provocative faith memoirs this year, Mark Richard's *House of Prayer No. 2* and Donna Johnson's *Holy Ghost Girl.* Speaking as one who will happily curl up in a hammock with the letters of Ignatius of Antioch, I think spiritual themes are pretty dang compelling. But Richard and Johnson actually have the edge on Ignatius. They really know how to move the story along.

ABOUT THE AUTHOR

Photo Credit: Shelley LaLonde

RHODA JANZEN is the author of the #1 *New York Times* bestselling *Mennonite in a Little Black Dress* and the poetry collection *Babel's Stair*. She holds a PhD from UCLA and teaches English and creative writing at Hope College.